THE BRITISH LIBRARY
writers' lives

George Gordon,
Lord Byron

I can not speak of love to thee

   Though thou art young, gay & free;

There is a spell thou dost not see

   What hides a genuine love

And not the spell in iron cant

   For thee to sigh a

   As truth itself abhorring a lie

3.

'ere dull a glare

   The woman's heart 'there

Admit not there love in for that

   others love all, near

Perchance tis for Friend, perchance

   But false or true thou canst tell

So much hast thou from all to fear

   In that unconcealable spell

THE BRITISH LIBRARY
writers' lives

George Gordon, **Lord Byron**

MARTIN GARRETT

OXFORD
UNIVERSITY PRESS

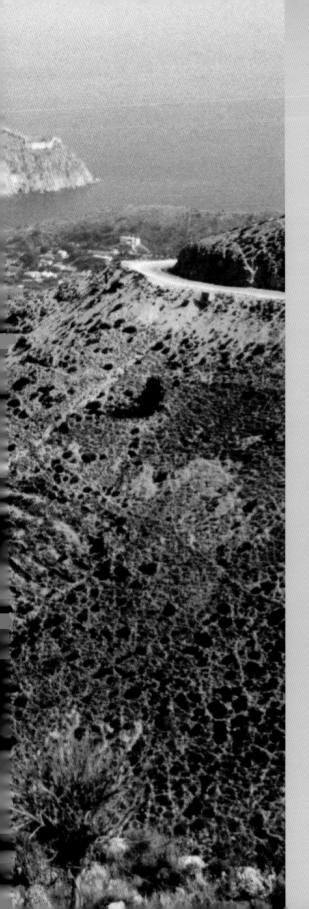

Contents

George Gordon, Lord Byron

*Maps of Great Britain,
right, and Europe,
below, showing places
where Byron lived or
visited.*

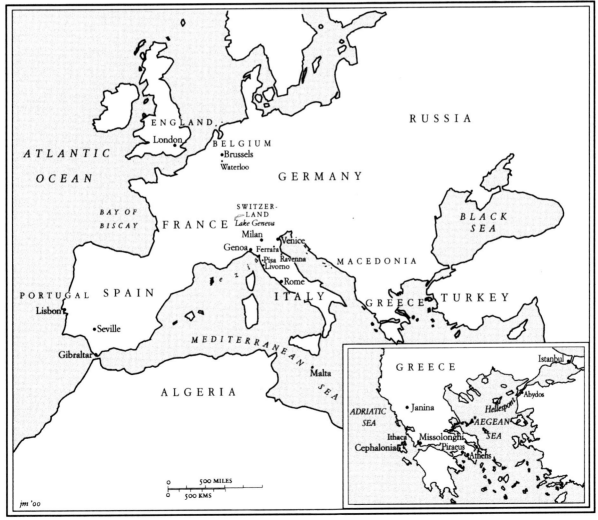

Introduction

'The great object of life is Sensation', Lord Byron declared to his future wife in September 1813:

> to feel that we exist, even though in pain. It is the 'craving void' which drives us to Gaming, to Battle, to Travel – to intemperate but keenly felt pursuits of every description whose principal attraction is the agitation inseparable from their accomplishment.

This craving for sensation could be explained in rather simple psychological terms: Byron needed to assert his identity having lost his (in any case unreliable) father in infancy or, he was lame and needed to prove himself just as active and able as others. It can also be explained more broadly as characteristic of its time. The writings of eighteenth-century philosophers, including Jean-Jacques Rousseau, had promoted the importance of individual feelings and sensibilities, and, at least at the beginning, the French Revolution and Napoleon Bonaparte had seemed to promise the fulfilment of such individual liberty. Disappointed at the more complicated reality of events, a number of English writers, including William Wordsworth, had turned their back on their own youthful 1790s faith in revolution and unfettered personal responses. Byron's generation, too young actually to have seen the revolution turn sour and not yet entirely convinced that Napoleon was more pragmatist than idealist, were readier to proclaim the power of 'sensation'.

Whichever explanation one prefers, Byron at times derived similar stimulus or 'agitation' from his many sexual relationships and, usually more lastingly, from writing poetry. This last was an activity which he insisted was inferior to military or political action. But he also insisted that it was inescapable: that it was 'the lava of the imagination whose eruption prevents an earthquake', preventing the poet simply going mad. He often expressed scepticism about the idea of poetry as a sacred calling – as it was, for instance, for Wordsworth – yet he experienced a similar compulsion to write it. Byron has joined the list of poets we usually call 'the Romantics' but he could be downright derisory about other Romantics and had boundless respect for the more classical 'Augustan' poets against whom they – and in practice he – were in many ways reacting.

Byron's life exhibited similar paradoxes. He participated in idealistic love and casual sex, was bisexual, by turns an ascetic and a libertine, idle and furiously productive, a religious sceptic who admired Roman Catholicism, an aristocrat and a republican. This extravagantly contradictory figure has always been the delight of biographers; more people have heard that he was 'mad, bad and dangerous to know' (as Lady Caroline Lamb put it) than have read the poems. But the work and the life need not be separate: the work often explores versions of Byron's own life and opinions, contradictions and all. Byron's best poems refuse to avoid paradox. And in thus refusing easy answers he is arguably as much a modern poet as a Romantic or an Augustan.

🌊 *Early Years*

The Byrons were well known for their recurrent financial problems, sexual promiscuity, and drinking. The 5th Lord, the poet's great-uncle, killed a fellow landowner in a drunken argument in 1765 and, judged guilty only of manslaughter by the House of Lords, withdrew to Newstead Abbey, his ancestral home in Nottinghamshire, where he presided over its steady dereliction and impoverishment. Once keen on bombarding model boats on the lake at Newstead with a small cannon, as he became poorer he was reduced to such amusements as keeping crickets and staging cockroach races. He disinherited his son for rejecting marriage with an heiress – the sort of woman the poet was to call 'a golden dolly' – in favour of a love-match with his equally poor cousin Juliana. The family fortunes ought to have revived when Juliana's brother Captain John Byron (1756-91) married two fairly 'golden' brides in succession – Amelia, Marchioness of Carmarthen, who died soon after the birth of their daughter, Augusta, in 1784, and in 1785 Catherine Gordon, an innocent young Scotswoman whom he met at Bath, centre of fashion and marriage-making.

Catherine Gordon, daughter of the 12th laird of Gight in Aberdeenshire, was very proud ('as haughty as Lucifer', said her son) of her descent from King James I of Scotland. More important, as far as her husband was concerned, was the £23,000 she brought him. He ran through much of it during their short marriage. Sometimes known as 'Mad Jack', he was an ex-army officer addicted to gambling, women, and high living. Mainly to avoid creditors, the couple moved several times between

Catherine Gordon Byron, the poet's mother, by Thomas Stewardson.

John Murray

England, France, and Scotland. (The ancestral estate at Gight soon had to be sold.) John Byron remained in France while Catherine gave birth to their son, the future lord and poet George Gordon Byron, at lodgings in Holles Street, London, on 22 January 1788. After this the captain appeared, intermittently, only in order to charm yet more money out of his wife. She protested violently at his foolishness but gave in; fortunately, knowing her own weakness, she had her remaining £4,222 of capital securely placed in the hands of trustees in March 1788. She grieved when the feckless husband died at Valenciennes, by dissipation or suicide, in 1791. But later, in her explosive moods, she would, says Byron, 'rake up the ashes of my father', abuse him and say, with strong Scottish emphasis, that her son would be 'a true Byrrone, which is the worst epithet she can invent'. George, who was two years old when he last encountered his father, later claimed 'I perfectly remember him; and had very early a horror of matrimony, from the sight of domestic broils' [quarrels].

Catherine Byron's black periods – mother and son too had their 'domestic broils' – were perhaps congenital but were exacerbated by her rather neglected childhood and troubled marriage and by her son's own wilfulness and love of mischief. People who knew Byron in Aberdeen, where he and his mother lived from 1789, remembered him pricking her fleshy arm with a pin as they sat in their pew at Old St Paul's Episcopal Chapel and interfering with a mill-wheel by 'pittin' bits o' sticks and orra things' in it. Bored during a visit to Lady Abercromby of Birkenbog, he put his coat and hat on a pillow and launched it from an upper room 'with a shriek ... in the hope of persuading his mother that he had accidentally fallen'. One reason for his need to let off steam in this way was his sensitivity about his lameness and the pain caused by attempts to treat it. There has been some debate about the exact nature of the condition, but we know that his right foot turned inward. Corrective footgear did little to help and perhaps even made matters worse. For much of his life he remained sensitive about the way he walked. As a child he allegedly shouted 'Dinna speak of it!' at a woman who had the temerity to allude to it; he had learnt more stoicism and more wit by the time he wrote, in 1811, that 'in another existence I expect to have *two* if not *four* legs by way of compensation'. Some have attributed Byron's melancholy, his sexual over-activity, or his poetic ability to his foot; more certainly there was a compensatory element in his passion for riding, boxing, and long-distance swimming.

After some limited early schooling, Byron was sent to Aberdeen Grammar School in 1794. The curriculum at this time consisted almost entirely of Latin; the rest of his education happened mostly at home. He read widely, liking especially history and the Old Testament, the whole of which he had apparently read by the age of eight. Richard Knolles' *General History of the Turks* (1603) was one of the works

which predisposed him towards his later interest in things eastern. Another legacy of these Scottish years was a love of mountains and waters. He retained in particular a strong impression of Lachin y Gair (or Lochnagar), with its 'eternal snows', towering 'so majestically above the rest of our *Northern Alps*'. The poem 'Lachin y Gair' included in Byron's *Hours of Idleness* (1807) dwells nostalgically on such scenes.

If Byron felt nostalgia for the land he left at the age of ten, he remembered with much more intense feeling his precocious love, possibly at the age of seven, for his cousin Mary Duff. 'I recollect all we said to each other, all our caresses, her features, my restlessness, sleeplessness....How the deuce did all this occur so early?'

Castle Street, Aberdeen, in 1812. In some moods the adult Byron dwelt fondly on the fact that he was 'half a Scot by birth, and bred/A whole one' (Don Juan, *X.17*).

The British Library 2370.b.4

West view of Newstead Abbey, c.1815. The 'grand arch ... once screen'd many an aisle' of the medieval abbey. (Don Juan, XIII.59).

Newstead Abbey

he wondered in his journal in 1813. 'I certainly had no sexual ideas for years afterwards; and yet my misery, my love for that girl were so violent, that I sometimes doubt if I have ever really been attached since'. Hearing later of her marriage 'was like a thunder-stroke – it nearly choked me'. Byron had sought, as often afterwards, an ideal love unlike his all-too-human relationship with his mother. Another early relationship proved more traumatic: starting when he was about nine, he explained to his friend Hobhouse, 'a free Scotch girl' – his nurse May Gray – 'used to come to bed to him and play tricks with his person'. This activity – now classifiable as child abuse – continued for perhaps two years until she was dismissed when the boy at last complained about her conduct (including 'perpetually beating him' when drunk) to John Hanson, the solicitor who looked after the Byrons' financial and other affairs.

Byron's life and his mother's changed suddenly when, in May 1798, he succeeded as 6th Lord Byron on the death of his great-uncle. The ten-year-old was,

at first, simply bewildered, bursting into tears when his title was solemnly read out at school. He had been heir since 1794, when the 5th Lord's grandson was killed in battle in Corsica, but had no contact with the old 'Wicked Lord' and was little prepared to mix in aristocratic circles. Mother and son, who experienced some difficulty in getting together sufficient money for the journey to Newstead Abbey, arrived there in August. The abbey, founded in the twelfth century, had been bought and converted by Sir John Byron of Colwick soon after Henry VIII's dissolution of the monasteries (1536-40). George Byron immediately loved the place for its lake, its rooms and grounds to wander in, its cloister and ghost stories, and its romantic ruins – the 'glorious remnant of the Gothic pile' mentioned in *Don Juan* canto 13. Later, Newstead gave him the chance to play the prosperous and well established seigneur who could show a younger school friend 'plenty of hunting, shooting, and fishing' at 'my seat in the country'. Even the unruined parts of the house, however,

Byron's bedroom at Newstead Abbey. He first came to live at Newstead when he was ten, in 1798.

Newstead Abbey

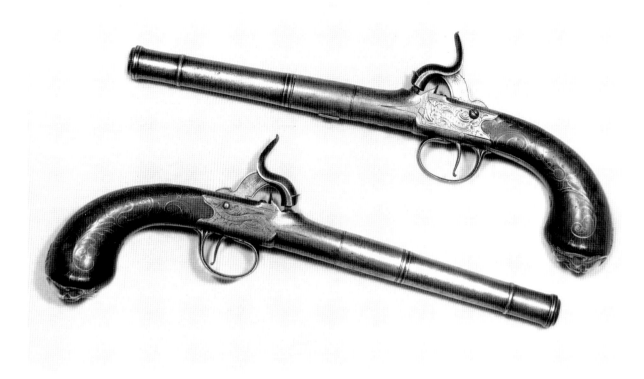

Pistols belonging to Byron. Although several times he came close to fighting a duel, his usual targets were bottles.

Newstead Abbey

were in a somewhat dilapidated condition and there was little furniture; the Great Hall – once it had been cleared of hay – was a good place for the young lord to practise firing his predecessor's pistols. With the family finances already precarious, the cost of repairs and refitting meant that for part of Byron's youth Newstead was rented out.

Lame, an outsider who spoke with a Scottish accent (some witnesses maintained that he never quite lost it), and lacking the money and connections of lords with more provident predecessors, Byron soon felt the need of gaining at least some dignity by means of education. In 1799, afraid of being 'branded with the name of a dunce', he petitioned his mother for a tutor. She arranged some further Latin tuition for him. A period at a small school in Dulwich followed and then, in 1801, entry to Harrow. (With Hanson's help Mrs Byron had obtained, as an impoverished noblewoman, a pension of £300 from the government. £500 a year for Byron's education now followed.) For several years he was lonely and unhappy in this great public school. In the early months of 1803 there was friction with his tutor, Henry Drury, who found him disruptive in class. For a time in 1803-4 he refused to return to school, at least partly in order to remain in the vicinity of Mary Chaworth of Annesley Hall, near Newstead. His unrequited love for this '*beau idéal* of all that my youthful fancy could paint of beautiful', two years older than he was, was made all the more romantic by the fact that she was the great-niece of the man killed by the 'Wicked Lord Byron'.

A portrait miniature of Mary Chaworth, with whom Byron was 'distractedly in love' when he was fifteen. She married Jack Musters soon afterwards. After the failure of this marriage she expressed greater interest in Byron, but it was not requited.

Newstead Abbey

Eventually, however, Byron came to respect the headmaster, his tutor's father, Dr Joseph Drury. Drury later explained to Byron's friend Thomas Moore how, observing the 'mind in his eye', he had understood that this seeming 'wild mountain colt' could 'be led by a silken string to a point, rather than by a cable'. When Drury retired in 1805 the mountain colt reasserted itself by leading a rebellion against the new headmaster, Dr Butler, even setting fire to his desk according to one account. But by this time Byron was well established at Harrow. No longer the solitary (if perhaps a little self-consciously poetic) youth often seen reclining on one of the graves in Harrow churchyard, he had a following – based to some extent on sexual attraction – among those a few years younger than himself. Byron's particular favourite was John Fitzgibbon, Earl of Clare, to whom he would address several poems, and who would bring back the intimate joys of that time in a brief encounter years later in Italy. They were, Byron noted in his journal, 'but five minutes together – and in the public road – but I hardly recollect an hour of my existence which could be weighed against them'.

Harrow, as a community with its own traditions, gave Byron a position, an identity safe from his mother, whose proximity he found increasingly difficult to bear. He could ask his half-sister, Augusta Byron, brought up in more decorous

15

aristocratic households, to come to his last Speech Day in 1805 in 'one of his Lordships most *dashing* carriages, as our Harrow *etiquette*, admits of nothing but the most *superb* vehicles, on our Grand *Festivals*'. At Speech Day (to which Augusta did not, in the event, come) Byron had the opportunity to perform, to engage in passionate display, but without complicated consequences or rejection, as he thundered out King Lear's 'Blow winds and crack your cheeks ...'

Byron went to Trinity College, Cambridge, in the autumn of 1805 and was no more impressed with the university's staid curriculum than were most of his contemporaries. (Reform did not begin in earnest until the 1850s.) Partly in order to explain his own habits and expenses, he told John Hanson that 'Study is the last pursuit of the Society; the Master eats, drinks, and sleeps; the Fellows *drink, dispute* and *pun*, the *employments* of the under Graduates you will probably conjecture without my description'. Later he kept a tame bear in a turret in the Great Court at Trinity; when 'they asked me what I meant to do with him ... my reply was "he should sit for Fellowship".' At first, certainly, he enjoyed the usual undergraduate sense of freedom, enhanced by £500 a year, a servant and a horse. But even greater liberty, and the money-lenders who could finance it, were available elsewhere and Byron, although he eventually managed to get himself awarded a degree, spent relatively

Trinity College, Cambridge. Byron's poem of 1805, 'Granta: a Medley', satirises Cambridge as a place of venal college fellows, 'unprofitable knowledge', and 'drunkenness and dice'.

The British Library 127.i.10

little time in Cambridge before leaving at the end of 1807. For most of his second term he was in London, going to the theatre, engaging in promiscuous sex, and learning to fence from the fashionable Henry Angelo and to box from the former champion John 'Gentleman' Jackson.

Back in Cambridge, however, Byron did make some of his most lasting friendships, notably with his loyal companion John Cam Hobhouse. And he formed a strong mutual attachment with the Trinity choirboy John Edleston, whom, he said in 1807, he loved 'more than any human being'. Edleston's parting gift when he left Cambridge to join, with Byron's help, 'an advantageous mercantile concern', was a small heart of cornelian (a semi-precious stone, now more often known as carnelian). In response Byron wrote 'The Cornelian'. Here the youth offers his gift 'with downcast look,/As fearful, that I might refuse it' and it seems to take its sparkling from a tear. Beneath the bravado and the gradually developing wit of Byron's letters and conversation this more sentimental strain persisted; only much later did he find ways of expressing cynicism and sentiment convincingly within a single work.

'The Cornelian' was included in *Fugitive Pieces* and *Poems on Various Occasions*, the volumes privately printed in the autumn of 1806 and January 1807 and much of which reappears in *Hours of Idleness* (1807), Byron's first published work.

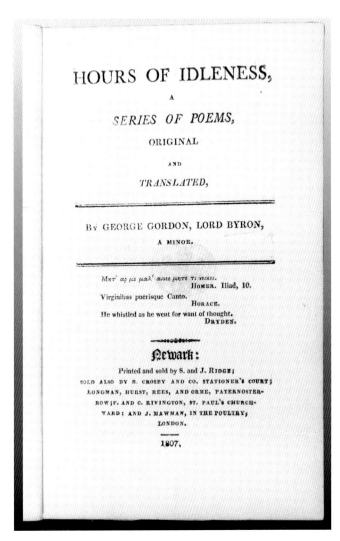

The title-page of Byron's first published work, Hours of Idleness, *1807. In the preface he states that 'These productions are the fruits of the lighter hours of a young man, who has lately completed his nineteenth year....To the dictates of young ambition, may be ascribed many actions more criminal, and equally absurd'.*

The British Library 11641.c.6

These collections of love poems, parodies, translations and nostalgic pieces on Harrow 'where friendships were form'd, too romantic to last', were, says the preface to *Hours of Idleness*, 'written on many, and various occasions', and at first 'intended merely for the perusal of a friendly circle'. Part of that circle, mainly in Southwell, the quiet Nottinghamshire cathedral town where Catherine Byron had been living since 1803, was shocked by some of the poems. In particular, respectable provincial readers could not approve of 'To Mary', which includes such sentiments as 'And smile to think, how oft we've done,/What prudes declare a sin to act is'. On the advice of Southwell mentors Byron suppressed *Fugitive Pieces* (only four copies have survived) and, by the removal of 'To Mary' and similar elements, produced what he asserted to be the 'miraculously chaste' *Poems on Various Occasions*. He did retain, in 'Childish Recollections', lines likely to cause offence elsewhere (but joy among Harrow schoolboys) by mocking his former headmaster Dr Butler as 'Pomposus'. But a reconciliation between Butler and Byron was brokered by Henry Drury and, somewhat shamefacedly, the poet suppressed the whole piece in the second edition of *Hours of Idleness*.

These inclusions and suppressions of material show Byron both willing to outrage and easily persuaded to conform. He regarded the poems mainly, he claimed, as a prelude to subsequent more serious achievement – he would obtain 'all the *Eclat*' of having 'published before I was 20' and then move on. But, as the wish for 'éclat' suggests, Byron did care a great deal about the way *Hours of Idleness* was received. Many reviews were favourable – *The Monthly Review* for November 1807, for instance, detected 'both ease and strength, both pathos and fire' – but *The Monthly Monitor* for January 1808 declared that he should have been whipped for these 'school exercises' and in May the powerful *Edinburgh Review* found his 'effusions' completely lifeless. The author was deeply wounded by the personal tone of these reviews. He had already – mainly in London in the intervals between carousing, excessive 'activity' with a blue-eyed sixteen-year-old called Caroline, and the resulting 'debility' – begun work on a satire of his fellow 'British Bards'. Now he converted this into the more comprehensively scathing *English Bards and Scotch Reviewers* (1809).

Part of Byron's corrected proof for the first printing of English Bards and Scotch Reviewers, *called at this point* British Bards. *The object of the satire in this poem is a duel which failed to take place between the critic Francis Jeffrey, founder of* The Edinburgh Review, *and the poet Thomas Moore, later Byron's friend.*

The British Library Egerton MS 2028 f.15v

The urgent need to write satire confirmed in Byron the taste he had already formed for the sane, epigrammatic, neo-classical flavour of late seventeenth- and eighteenth-century 'Augustan' poetry. He admired especially the sharply honed rhymed couplets of Alexander Pope (1688-1744). Conversely, and not unusually among educated readers of the day, he had an antipathy for the 'Lake Poets' of the generation before his own, William Wordsworth, Robert Southey, and Samuel Taylor Coleridge. In fact Byron would achieve renown both as a poet of feeling, not unlike the Lake Poets, and as an incisive satirist although in a rather different, less classical mode to Pope.

In *English Bards* Byron lashed out at so many people that he was to spend years apologising for his youthful intemperance to individuals whom he had misunderstood or later grew to appreciate. By 1816, at least in some moods, he regarded the poem as a 'miserable record of misplaced anger and indiscriminate acrimony'. But it was a useful vehicle for the wit hitherto directed mainly into letters and conversation. 'Fools are my theme, let Satire be my song' proclaims the poem with as much zest as anger; 'Behold! in various throngs the scribbling crew,/For notice eager, pass in long review' including the tribe of Scottish critics, 'Apollo's venal son' Walter Scott (later much admired by Byron), and the prosaic Wordsworth, hero of his own poem 'The Idiot Boy'. The poet pleads with Southey to 'cease thy varied song!/ A Bard may chaunt too often, and too long'; more colloquially he begs Rev. William Bowles, who has dared to write against Pope, 'Stick to thy sonnets, man, at least they sell'. Many victims were added in the second edition and the poem

Byron's memorial to his dog, Boatswain, in the grounds of Newstead Abbey. For a time Byron intended to be buried next to him.

Newstead Abbey

continued to sell apace until in 1812, persuaded mainly by Henry Fox, Lord Holland, Byron suppressed the fifth edition. (In *English Bards* at Holland House objectionable 'Scotchmen feed, and Critics may carouse' but in 1812 Byron himself was often to be seen at this centre of Whig politics.) Even then the publisher, Cawthorne, went on printing more versions up to 1819.

Byron spent the autumn of 1808 at Newstead, ordering expensive redecoration, fathering a son by his maid Lucy – he made adequate financial provision for her and the child – and entertaining friends. John Cam Hobhouse, Charles Skinner Matthews and others gathered for a house-party where they paid irreverent tribute to Newstead's monastic origins: 'I had got a famous cellar, and monks' dresses from a masquerade warehouse', Byron recalled. 'We ... used to sit up late in our friars' dresses, drinking burgundy, claret, champagne, and what not, out of the *skull-cup*, and all sorts of glasses, and buffooning all around the house, in our conventual [monastic] garments.' The cup made from a skull found in the grounds at Newstead has done much for Byron's satanic reputation, but his own attitude to the macabre specimen could be more light-hearted: 'In me behold the only skull,' he has it say, 'From which, unlike a living head,/Whatever flows is never dull' ('Lines inscribed upon a Cup formed from a Skull', 1808).

But he could still be sentimental as often as he was outrageous. When his Newfoundland dog Boatswain died suddenly in November 1808 he wrote a poem commemorating his unswerving loyalty and friendship, later to be the inscription for the monument still in the gardens at Newstead, of one

> *Who possessed beauty without Vanity,*
> *Strength without Insolence,*
> *Courage without Ferocity,*
> *And all the Virtues of Man without his Vices.*

People could rarely be counted on as Boatswain could. Byron's guardian Lord Carlisle, for instance, declined to stand as Byron's sponsor for admission to the House of Lords after his twenty-first birthday in 1809 and accordingly found himself pilloried in *English Bards* for faults including his 'paralytic puling' [whining] in verse.

❧ *Byron's Grand Tour*

For much of the eighteenth century young British aristocratic men (and increasing numbers of the wealthier gentry) made their 'Grand Tour' of Europe together with their tutors or 'bear-leaders'. The aim was to expand and polish their hitherto rather narrow education and to acquaint them with foreign languages, manners, art, architecture, and antiquities. Even if the reality was often more prosaic, travellers usually brought back with them a store of anecdotes, a cosmopolitan air and some drawings and water-colours of the sights.

It is difficult to imagine Byron treading dutifully behind a bear-leader or copying paintings in Florence, but he was always anxious to do things befitting his rank, and the tradition of titled travel appealed for a number of more personal reasons too. He wanted to get away from both his loving but volatile and embarrassing mother and from his debts. Byron and his friend Hobhouse were able to set off on their tour only with the aid of a loan of more than £6000 raised by their Cambridge friend Scrope Berdmore Davies from a mixture of winnings at the gambling-table and borrowings from money-lenders. Bored in the provinces and unable to avoid sinking into dissipation in London – but equally, perhaps, hoping to try fresh foreign pleasures – Byron sought a new beginning. And going abroad was also a way of leaving behind his intense and potentially scandalous relationship with the Cambridge choirboy Edleston.

The Grand Tour had changed markedly in recent years because its traditional destinations, including Italy, were in the hands of a hostile power, Napoleon Bonaparte's France. Those venturesome enough still to take the Tour increasingly went further afield – Byron, having

John Cam Hobhouse (1786-1869), Byron's loyal friend and posthumous defender. Following his travels with Byron he wrote A Journey Through Albania *(1813).*

The British Library 841.m.18

toyed with the idea of Persia or India, eventually chose Greece and Turkey. Classical Greece was familiar in the reading of the educated classes but in modern times it had been visited by the bolder travellers only. Turkey too, although known as the centre of the once hugely powerful empire which frightened and fascinated Christian Europe, was still visited by relatively few westerners. On the way there it would be possible to take in Portugal, Spain, and Malta. What Byron did not expect was that the journey would lead him to write one of the best-selling works of the nineteenth century and confirm him, for all his protestations of the worthlessness of that calling, as a poet.

Hobhouse and Byron sailed from Falmouth for Lisbon on 2 July 1809. They found Portugal 'in a state of disorder', with a major battle between the English and the French about to happen in Spain: at Talavera on 28-29 July Sir Arthur Wellesley, later Duke of Wellington, achieved one of his most notable victories. The battle would find its way into *Childe Harold's Pilgrimage* canto one (1812) where, in one of Byron's many reflections on the futility of war, the rival armies meet 'To feed the crow on Talavera's plain,/And fertilize the field that each pretends to claim'. But at the time possible danger and war were part of the excitement and newness of the first days abroad. Enthusiasm shows through Byron's facetious letter to a friend on 16 July: 'I am very happy here, because I loves oranges, and talk bad Latin to the monks, who understand it, as it is like their own, – and I goes into society (with my pocket-pistols), and I swims in the Tagus all across at once' – a deliberately casual reference to the considerable feat of swimming, in spite of wind and currents, from old Lisbon to Belem Castle – 'and swears Portuguese, and have got a diarrhoea, and bites from the mosquitoes.' When he finally managed to send from Gibraltar the longer and more eloquent equivalent of a back-packer's postcard to his mother on 11 August, he told her about the beauties 'of every description natural and artificial' of the village of Cintra near Lisbon with its 'palaces and gardens rising in the midst of rocks, cataracts, and precipices, convents on stupendous heights'.

After ten days in Lisbon, Byron and Hobhouse spent a week riding to Seville and from there after a few days to Cadiz. Still the traveller abroad for the first time, he swooned over Spanish women with 'Long black hair, dark languishing eyes, *clear* olive complexions, and forms more graceful in motion than can be conceived by an

Englishman used to the drowsy listless air of his countrywomen'. But it was not until he reached Malta at the end of August that he actually became seriously involved with a woman, Constance Spencer Smith. He was fascinated partly by her romantic adventures: the daughter and wife of diplomats in Constantinople, she told him the story of her narrow escapes from Napoleonic pursuers in Italy. They knew each other for less than three weeks, but they contemplated running away together and he nearly fought a duel because of her. Soon after bloodshed had been averted by an apology from the captain whose insinuations had offended him, Byron left for Greece on the brig *Spider* and so 'escaped murder and adultery'. On his side at least the passion was strong but temporary. It was, tradition has it, the subject of the short poem he wrote in Athens in January 1810 beginning 'The spell is broke, the charm is flown!' (Soon after their parting she had figured in verse as 'Sweet Florence'.)

The Scottish novelist John Galt (1779-1839), a fellow passenger of Byron and Hobhouse from Gibraltar to Malta, recalled his first impressions:

> *Byron held himself aloof, and sat on the rail, leaning on the mizzen shrouds, inhaling, as it were, poetical sympathy, from the gloomy Rock [of Gibraltar], then dark and stern in the twilight. There was in all about him that evening much waywardness; he spoke petulantly to Fletcher, his valet; and was evidently ill at ease with himself, and fretful towards others. I thought he would turn out an unsatisfactory shipmate; yet there was something redeeming in the tones of his voice, when, some time after he had indulged his sullen meditation, he again addressed Fletcher; so that, instead of finding him ill-natured, I was soon convinced he was only capricious.*

(William Fletcher, from Newstead, hated foreign travel, but remained with his master during almost all his journeys and was with him when he died.) On about the third day 'Byron relented from his rapt mood, as if he felt it was out of place, and became playful'; to pass the time, the passengers joined in his favourite sport of firing pistols at bottles. But then again, the evening before they reached Cagliari in Sardinia, 'he made himself a man forbid, took his station on the railing ... and there, for hours, sat in silence, enamoured, it may be, of the moon'.

Had Galt seen or heard no more of Byron after Cagliari, he 'should have retained a much more favourable recollection of Mr Hobhouse; ... for he was a cheerful companion, full of odd and droll stories ... good-humoured and intelligent – altogether an advantageous specimen of a well-educated English gentleman'. These qualities in Hobhouse helped relieve a 'nervous dejection' in Galt and usefully balanced Byron's more wayward tendencies, but one can see that Byron's mysteriousness might have been more appealing to 'Florence'. Soon it would be enticing thousands as, in spite of his initial denials, readers identified the melancholy Childe Harold with his creator. (A 'childe' is a candidate for knighthood.)

Greece

Fair Greece! sad relic of departed worth!
Immortal, though no more! though fallen, great!
Who now shall lead thy scatter'd children forth,
And long accustomed bondage uncreate?

Greece had been subject to the rule of the Ottoman Turks for four centuries. This, many western Europeans concluded, was the fault of the servile modern Greeks, unworthy successors of the brave and cultured ancients who could still be admired in their literature and the ruins of their temples. Byron, at times at least, agreed with this view: even if Greece could be liberated by foreign intervention its people would remain a 'degenerate horde', 'hereditary bondsmen'. Yet there had always been those who believed, either from observation or as an abstract article of faith, that the Greeks could recover their ancient strength. Byron had read widely in the poets and travellers – both those who scorned the modern Greeks and those who held out hopes for them – and many of the sentiments expressed in *Childe Harold's Pilgrimage*, canto two, would have been unsurprising to eighteenth-century readers. What is distinctive, however, is the intensity and immediacy of response to the landscape, ruins, myths, history and people of the 'land of lost gods and godlike men'.

At first Byron was less interested in the Greeks than in their overlords. He was fascinated, above all, by the prospect of meeting the ogreish Ali Pasha, who had

fought, schemed and bought his way from a minor Albanian chieftainship to the effective rule (nominally subject to the Sultan) of much of modern Albania and north-western and central Greece. And so, a few days after landing at Patras on 26 September 1809, the travellers set off to ride to Ali's capital, Janina, passing with Childe Harold over 'many a mount sublime,/Through lands scarce notic'd in historic tales', non-classical places whose unfamiliarity was one of the many factors which would contribute to the popularity of the poem.

Janina, since its capture by Ali in 1787, had become in most respects a pleasant and peaceable town. Hobhouse later remembered its 'houses, domes, and minarets, glittering though gardens of orange and lemon trees' and its lake-island. To meet the pasha himself, however, it was necessary to go on north through the mountains to Tebelene, his original Albanian home, from which he had been conducting, it was explained, 'a little war'. The prospect of coming face to face with this man who roasted enemies on spits must have been somewhat intimidating; as they approached Janina the travellers had come upon a severed arm hanging from a tree. But Ali, forever playing the French and English off against each other in the hope of territorial or financial gain for himself, was happy to receive English visitors, and took a particular interest in Byron, who wrote to his mother that the old man was 'certain I was a man of birth because I had small ears, curling hair, and little white hands'. Ali said he should consider him as his father during his visit 'and indeed he treated me like a child, sending me almonds and sugared sherbet, fruits and sweetmeats 20 times a day. – He begged me to visit him often, and at night when he was more at leisure'. (Clearly his feelings were more than paternal.) Byron and Hobhouse were impressed by the apparent gentleness and courtesy of this well known killer. He was later an influence on such savage but polite figures as the pirate-chief Lambro in Byron's *Don Juan*. The pasha is described more directly in *Childe Harold's Pilgrimage*, which was probably begun in Tebelene.

The Lake Island of Janina, where the seemingly invincible Ali Pasha died in a hail of bullets in 1822 at the end of a war with his overlord, the Sultan.

The British Library 841.m.18

The 'degenerate' Greeks seemed likely to remain enslaved by rulers as savage and successful as Ali. But this impression began to be modified, importantly for the future, when the travellers, having reached the northern Peloponnese, met Andreas Londos, a young Greek Cogia Basha, or provincial governor, in December 1809. Hobhouse says that when they mentioned Constantine Rigas of Velestino, who, as Byron later put it, 'perished in the attempt to revolutionize Greece' in 1798, Londos jumped up suddenly, knocked over the chess board on which he and Hobhouse had been playing, 'and clasping his hands, repeated the name of the patriot with a thousand passionate exclamations, the tears streaming down his cheeks'. An appendix to *Childe Harold* includes a translation of Rigas' 'Battle Hymn'.

Next came a detour to Delphi (mostly unexcavated at the time), where they scratched their names on a pillar near the traditional site of the Castalian Spring which, a classical education assured them, was the fount of poetic inspiration. And then, late in December, they proceeded to Athens. The future Greek capital and former city-state was, depending on which aspect was emphasised, a squalid or picturesque place, more a large village than a city. But the Acropolis still gleamed over all, Byron and Hobhouse lived on friendly terms with the inhabitants, and later Byron told his mother that Athens was 'a place which I think I prefer upon the whole to any I have seen'. One thing, however, made him angry, like many a later philhellene (Greek sympathiser) and like more Greeks at the time than used to be supposed: the affair of the 'Elgin Marbles'. There was keen rivalry between the British and the French to remove from the Parthenon its frieze, said to be the work of the ancient sculptor Phidias and depicting the procession at the great festival of Panathenaia. Some of these 'marbles' had been obtained by Lord Elgin in 1802 and subsequently displayed in London. (They are still, controversially, in the British Museum.) Byron had been unimpressed by them; these 'Phidian freaks,/Misshapen monuments and maim'd antiques' found a place in *English Bards and Scotch Reviewers*. But having experienced Greece and seen the depredation first-hand, he attacked Elgin not for his taste but for his activities as a despoiler, both in *Childe Harold* canto two and the more virulent *The Curse of Minerva*, begun in Athens in March 1811. Ironically Byron, with the then unfinished manuscript of this poem, left Athens for the last time on the same ship which was carrying most of the remaining marbles.

During the first visit to Athens the travellers lodged in a house belonging to a widow, Tarsia Makri, who lived in the adjoining house with her three adolescent daughters. Lemon-trees in the courtyard provided, Hobhouse noted, 'the fruit that seasoned the pilaf'; the youngest daughter, Teresa, provided the myth of the Maid of Athens. Aged only about twelve, she was dignified with this appelation in the lyric 'Maid of Athens, ere we part,/Give, oh give me back my heart ...' Apparently, Byron later told Hobhouse, her mother 'was mad enough to imagine I was going to marry the girl' or at least pay money for her. Teresa herself, interviewed years later by an American naval officer, said that the tale of their love 'was, in plain Turkish, all bosh – humbug'. (During his time in Greece Byron seems to have reserved his deeper, sometimes unrequited, affections for boys and young men.)

Teresa Makri, Byron's 'Maid of Athens', as depicted by an artist in 1812 and featured in the book Byron Beauties, *1836.*

The British Library 11661.t.20

In March 1810 the travellers crossed the Aegean to Smyrna (Izmir), where the first draft of canto two – the Greek section – of *Childe Harold* was completed. On 11 April they sailed again, on the frigate *Salsette*, for Constantinople. They paused to pay their respects to the place then generally regarded as the site of Homer's Troy – really the much later remains of Alexandria Troas. And on 3 May Byron performed the same feat as had the mythological Leander for the sake of his beloved Hero, swimming across the Hellespont from Sestos to Abydos. Winds and currents made for a swim of up to four miles, which took Lieutenant Ekenhead of the *Salsette* an hour and five minutes and Byron five minutes longer. It was celebrated by Byron, humorously but persistently, in numerous letters, a short poem written soon afterwards, and canto two of *Don Juan*, where the agile hero

> *could, perhaps, have pass'd the Hellespont,*
> *As once (a feat on which ourselves we prided)*
> *Leander, Mr Ekenhead, and I did.*

It was a characteristically Byronic gesture, a crossing of the frontier between fact and fiction. For on the one hand it was a real deed – one on which, he only half-jestingly told Francis Hodgson, 'I plume myself ... more than I could possibly do on any kind of glory, political, poetical, or rhetorical'. And on the other hand he could not resist working variations on it in prose and verse, and he had undertaken the whole exploit because of a story told by the Roman poet Ovid. He enacted his schoolroom reading and yoked ancient myth to his own growing legend.

Byron's poetry and his personal myth were also affected by an incident which occurred after his return to Athens from Constantinople in the summer of 1810. (Hobhouse left reluctantly for England at this point.) As he was riding near Piraeus he came upon a group of Turkish soldiers who were taking a young woman, sewn in a sack, to be drowned – the penalty for being caught in an act of 'illicit love'. Byron boldly threatened the party with a pistol – perhaps surprisingly, the often 'rapt' poet could usually be relied upon to act decisively in a crisis. He persuaded them to return to the governor, who, on payment of an undisclosed sum, agreed to let the woman go. Whether or not, as is often supposed, Byron himself had been her lover, three years later he wrote in his journal that he still found it difficult to describe and *'icy* even to recollect' his feelings at the time of this incident. In the intense, deliberately fragmented poem founded on it, *The Giaour* (meaning 'the infidel' and pronounced 'jowr'), Leila's Christian lover is too late to save her and the sack disappears with horrible inevitability – 'Sullen it plunged, and slowly sank,/The calm wave rippled to the bank'. *The Giaour*, Anne Barton points out in 'Byron and the Mythology of Fact', functions as an exorcism; 'in visualizing this catastrophe down to the last, grim detail Byron obtained a curious sense of relief. He had forced a ghost to materialize and to identify itself clearly as fiction, a creature of the imagination, not of fact'.

The Franciscan (Capuchin) Convent, Athens, founded in the seventeenth century, where Byron lived in 1810-11. Most of the building burnt down in 1821, except for the ancient, rounded structure towards the right of the picture, known as the Lantern of Demosthenes.

On the whole life in Athens in 1810-11 was more tranquil. The absence of the more sober Hobhouse allowed a certain sense of freedom. Byron's own sober activities in Athens in 1810-11 included a more thorough study than hitherto of 'the Romaic or Modern Greek language', an appendix on which was included in *Childe Harold*. He was living at the small Capuchin monastery which incorporated the ancient structure known because of its shape as the Lantern of Demosthenes. (In fact it has no connection with the Athenian orator Demosthenes but is a monument put up by a certain Lysicrates.) The abbot also ran a small school for six teenage boys on the premises, and Byron had much fun, horseplay and perhaps a degree of sexual dalliance with them. He wrote to Francis Hodgson on 20 January 1811 of some of the other joys of Athens:

> *Hymettus before me, the Acropolis behind, the temple of Jove [Olympieion] to my right, the town to the left, eh, Sir; there's a situation, there's your picturesque! nothing like that, Sir, in Lunnun, no not even the Mansion House. And I feed upon woodcocks and red mullet every day; and I have three horses ... and I ride to the Piraeus, and Phalerum.*

Opposite:

Byron in Albanian dress in Thomas Phillips' later version of his original painting of 1814. This has become one of the best known images of the poet. The outfit itself is now in the Museum of Costume in Bath.

National Portrait Gallery

~ *Politics, women and fame 1811-16*

Byron returned to England in July 1811, after just over two years' absence, to unpaid debts, an uncertain future, and unexpected bereavement. While still organising himself in London before going to Newstead, he 'heard one day' that his mother was seriously ill, 'the next of her death!' on 1 August, he told John Pigot, an old Southwell friend. Inevitably now, for all their past quarrels, he felt deeply the loss of her unequivocal love. Soon afterwards he learnt that Charles Skinner Matthews had died on or near the river Cam (almost certainly it was suicide); from Newstead he wrote to Scrope Davies that 'some curse hangs over me and mine. My mother lies a corpse in this house: one of my best friends is drowned in a ditch'. Just before this Byron had heard of the death of a friend from Harrow days, John Wingield. Worse was to come: in October came news that John Edleston had died of tuberculosis five months earlier. Byron commemorated him in verse as the safely female 'Thyrza'.

The 'curse' on 'me and mine' had a wider effect on the tone and structure of *Childe Harold* cantos one and two as Byron revised them for publication. The omission of flippant and satirical passages helped to emphasize elements of melancholy and meditation, and there was a clearer focus on the idea that civilization was in decline. It became all the more likely that readers would fuse Harold the melancholy wanderer with Byron the intriguingly melancholy poet.

Just before the publication of these cantos, which made his name as a poet, Byron performed on a different public stage. On

27 February 1812 he made his maiden speech in the House of Lords. Once he had been anxious to distance himself from party political adherence; but without allies he could not embark on the serious political career for which, he had sometimes told himself and others, his foreign tour was a preparation. And there were other factors which now disposed him publicly to identify himself with the Whig opposition unofficially led by Lord Holland. At Christmas 1811 he had seen and been appalled by the situation and treatment of Nottinghamshire stocking weavers ('frame workers') who, put out of work by new labour practices, were resorting to smashing other workers, or employers' frames. (Machine-breaking in the rapidly industrialising midlands and north of England reached its height at this period. Because one of the breakers was named Ned Ludd they became known as 'Luddites'.) Byron's speech was against the Tory government's bill to impose the death penalty for frame-breaking. He 'spoke very violent sentences with a sort of modest insolence', he told Francis Hodgson a week later, and with a degree of radicalism potentially embarrassing to the more moderate Whigs. He referred sarcastically to 'the capital crime of poverty', ridiculed ramshackle military moves against the unemployed workers, and – the tide was turning against Napoleon – pointed to the folly of enjoying foreign triumphs 'in the midst of domestic calamity'. Although the government bill succeeded in the end, he had made his mark as an orator of some promise and, incidentally, whetted interest in the *Childe Harold* cantos, published in early March. (He spoke again in the Lords on 21 April in support of the General Petition of the Roman Catholics of Ireland for full and equal civil rights.)

Byron had already begun to move in literary society; most importantly, in November 1811 he had met Samuel Rogers, the rich former banker whose rather traditional poetry he admired and had even praised in the

Opposite page:

Byron's maiden speech in support of the Nottinghamshire 'frame-breakers', as written out a few days before he delivered it in the House of Lords on 27 February 1812: 'are there not capital punishments sufficient in your statutes? is there not blood enough upon your penal code? that more must be poured forth to ascend to heaven and testify against you?'

British Library, Egerton MS 2030 f.4v

Left:

Samuel Rogers (1763-1855), the well known poet and former banker, whom Byron met in 1811. Portrait by Sir Thomas Lawrence.

The British Library 841.m.18

Opposite page left:

Byron's first fair copy of the opening of Childe Harold's Pilgrimage. *In the second stanza 'Burun' – a version of his own name – is heavily crossed out and replaced by 'Harold'. Later, he added an introductory stanza addressing the muse of poetry.*

John Murray

usually abusive *English Bards and Scotch Reviewers*. At Rogers' house he also met the Irish poet Thomas Moore, who had fared so much less well in *English Bards* that he had come close to fighting a duel with Byron, but who now became a close friend. According to Rogers there was some embarrassment at dinner because Byron steadily refused offers of soup, fish, mutton and wine and professed to eat 'Nothing but hard biscuits and soda-water', in the absence of which he was prepared to accept 'potatoes bruised down on his plate and drenched with vinegar'. (It is probably not true, as the notoriously malicious Rogers claimed, that after his potatoes the poet went off for 'a hearty meat-supper' at 'a club in St James's Street'.) Throughout his life Byron went through periods of radical dieting. He knew the after-effects of dissipation and was determined, like many a modern 'celebrity', to stay thin enough to correspond with his self-image and public reputation. Apparently he did make the desired impression on Moore, who remembered being at once struck with his gentleness of voice and manner, his 'glossy, curling and picturesque hair' and 'the pure, spiritual paleness of his features, in the expression of which, when he spoke, there was a perpetual play of lively thought, though melancholy was their habitual character when in repose'.

Possible explanations for the extraordinarily rapid commercial success of *Childe Harold* include Byron's political and literary contacts, public interest in the war in Spain alluded to in canto one, and human interest in the spiritually pale twenty-three-year-old author and his picturesque hair. The first edition of 500 expensive quarto copies sold out in a few days. (Between 1812 and 1816 nine cheaper editions followed.) Largely as a result of this huge and unexpected success Byron's new publisher John Murray, operating at this time in Fleet Street, was able to move to superior personal and business accommodation at 50 Albemarle Street, in the fashionable area of West London in which Byron himself often lived. The author, however, did not reap the financial benefits of the poem's success. As with a number of other works, he had given the copyright of the poem to his friend and distant relation Robert Charles Dallas. This was an act both of generosity and of snobbery – there was a tradition that literary earnings were beneath the dignity of a nobleman. Some modern commentators have, understandably, pointed out that the money could have been used to pay some of Byron's large outstanding tradesmen's bills. He

told himself, however, that soon he would be rich and then all debts could easily be settled; in the summer of 1812 he agreed, as he had sworn he never would, to put Newstead on the market and accepted an offer of £140,000 from Thomas Claughton. But Claughton changed his mind, eventually paying a forfeit of £25,000 in 1814, and the abbey was sold only after many further delays and expenses in 1817.

When the two *Childe Harold* cantos were published, Byron told Moore, 'I awoke one morning and found myself famous'. The world, said Rogers, went 'stark mad about Childe Harold and Byron'. He found himself much in demand, besieged by invitations, essential to the success of high-society gatherings, and especially popular with women. Having read the new poem Lady Caroline Lamb, the impulsive, intelligent, obsessive wife of William Lamb (later, as Lord Melbourne, prime minister under Queen Victoria) was desperate to meet the author. Seeing him

Childe Harold leaves his father's hall, in an 1814 engraving in Poetical Works of Lord Byron, *1847. 'Apart he stalk'd in joyless reverie, And from his native land resolv'd to go And visit scorching climes beyond the sea; With pleasure drugg'd, he almost longed for woe.'*

The British Library 11658.h.14

37

Richard Chamberlain as an unsympathetic but romantic Lord Byron in Robert Bolt's 1972 film Lady Caroline Lamb.

Canal + Image, U.K. Ltd

surrounded by other women at a ball she turned and left, but she had whetted his interest. He appeared to her to be excitingly 'mad, bad, and dangerous to know'; not long after Lady Holland had introduced them an affair began which was to cost both lovers much more pain than pleasure. Byron was attracted by Lady Caroline's originality, daring, and flattering belief in his genius, and the fact that, unlike his earlier lovers, she was of high social rank. She was, he told her at the beginning of their relationship, 'the cleverest most agreeable, absurd, amiable, perplexing, dangerous fascinating little being that lives now or ought to have lived 2000 years ago'. Stimulating perhaps, but worrying from the start, was her 'total want of common conduct' – her willingness to flout social propriety, to adopt unconvincing disguise as a page-boy, to embarrass him in public. It was he who, after a few months, broke with her in the late summer of 1812. She, however, did not agree with him that

Lady Caroline Lamb (1785-1828), by Mary Anne Knight. From childhood she was intelligent, restless, and unconventional. Most of her husband's family ostracised her during and after her affair with Byron in 1812. She eventually separated from her husband in 1825.

Newstead Abbey

this was simply one of the '1000 previous fancies of the same kind' they had both experienced. For many months she wrote letters; she sought opportunities to confront him in person, forged his handwriting in order to acquire a portrait of him from Murray, had young white-clad girls dance round a fire while she threw his letters into it. Later, in 1816, she published her novel *Glenarvon*, in which the evidently Byronic Glenarvon is both romantic hero and, under the alias Count Viviani, a murderer.

Byron's next substantial liaison, in 1812-13, was with the more equable – but confident and forceful – forty-year-old Jane Harley, Countess of Oxford. Herself influential in opposition circles, she encouraged him to take up again the 'Senatorial duties' neglected amid his literary fame and hectic love. He spoke a third and final

time in the House of Lords on 1 June 1813 to present the petition of Major John Cartwright, a campaigner for the radical reform of parliament. Again, as Byron was by now aware, he was ruling out a political career by the extremism of the views he espoused. (Reform of the voting system would begin only in the freer political climate of the 1830s; his own direct – as opposed to poetical – contribution to liberal causes would come now only in Italy and Greece.)

Caroline Lamb's mother-in-law, Lady Melbourne, was, in her different way, as important to Byron as was Lady Oxford. It was she who had acted as his principal confidante in his difficulties with Lady Caroline and she who became his intermediary with another, very different young woman, Lady Melbourne's niece Annabella Milbanke. In every way Annabella was unlike most of the women who flocked around Byron in his years of acclaim; quiet, learned – a fairly accomplished poet, interested in mathematics – the adored only child of rich elderly parents. She was confident in her own judgements. She found Byron, when they met in spring 1812, complex and fascinating, lacking 'that calm benevolence which could only touch my heart' but 'very handsome' and with manners 'in a superior degree such as one should attribute to Nature's gentleman'. He was also immediately interested in this 'very extraordinary girl' – 'who would imagine', he wondered, having read her poems, 'so much strength and variety of thought under that placid countenance?' 'I never saw a woman whom I *esteemed* so much' he told Lady Melbourne. Seeking to be rid of Caroline Lamb's attentions once and for all and tempted by the prospect of a family connection with Melbourne, whose company and friendship he so greatly enjoyed, he proposed to Milbanke through Melbourne in October 1812 and was rejected.

Opposite page:

John Hoppner's portrait of Jane Elizabeth, Countess of Oxford, in 1797. Byron found her intellectually as well as physically stimulating but was much less politically committed than she was. Breaking up with her, when she and her husband went abroad in 1813, caused him more regret than the end of many of his relationships.

Tate Gallery

Miniature of Annabella Milbanke, the future Lady Byron.

Reproduced by permission of the Keepers and Governors of Harrow School

Augusta Leigh (1784-1851), Byron's half-sister and lover. Byron explores his feelings for her in 'Stanzas for Music' (1814):
'Too brief for our passion, too long for our peace/ Were those hours – can their joy or their bitterness cease?/ We repent, we abjure, we will break from our chain,–/ We will part, we will fly to – unite it again!'
Portrait by Sir John Hayter.

British Museum

By the summer of 1813, although he often claimed to feel relief at not having married, he had all the more reason to wonder whether Milbanke and marriage might not protect him from other problems; in particular, he was now sexually involved with his half-sister Augusta, since 1807 the wife of Colonel George Leigh. In April 1814 Byron told Lady Melbourne (largely unshockable but in this case worried for him) that 'it is utterly impossible I can be so well liked elsewhere, and I have been all my life trying to make someone love me, and never got the sort

I preferred before'. Augusta, he would long maintain, was his one true love. But in the long term fear of public exposure rather cooled her feelings; and on his side their periods together alternated with bouts of depression, bad dreams, renewed dissipation and dieting. To her he wrote in May 1814 'Stanzas for Music': 'I speak not, I trace not, I breathe not thy name/ There is grief in the sound, there were guilt in the fame...'

Such tortured feelings found a more extended outlet in his Oriental Tales and the journal he kept between November 1813 and April 1814. The journal, like those Byron occasionally kept in later years, is full of insights into himself, others, books, full of attempts to do justice to the real complexity of being and self:

Byron's inkstand and candle holder. 'But words are things, and a small drop of ink Falling, like dew, upon a thought, produces That which makes thousands, perhaps millions, think.' (Don Juan, III.88).

Newstead Abbey

43

George Gordon, Lord Byron

Zuleika offers a rose to Selim: a Victorian impression of The Bride of Abydos, *from* The Illustrated Byron, *1854.*

The British Library
11611.k.3

This journal is a relief. When I am tired – as generally I am – out comes this, and down goes every thing. But I can't read it over; – and God knows what contradictions it may contain. If I am sincere with myself (but I fear one lies more to oneself than to anyone else), every page should confute, refute, and utterly abjure its predecessor.

While this avowed changeableness must be taken into account, it is probably true that, as the journal says, writing *The Bride of Abydos* in November 1813 was a therapeutic exercise: 'had I not done something at that time, I must have gone mad, by eating my own heart – bitter diet!' Already, in the summer, he had compulsively revised *The Giaour*. The original 407 lines became 685 in the first edition; by the seventh edition there were 1,334. Like that poem, *The Bride* explores extreme emotions in an oriental setting – safer, more distanced from personal fact than the novel and play Byron apparently tried, abortively, to write at this time. The poem deals with the doomed love of Selim and Zuleika, who in the first draft were half-brother and half-sister. In the published poem they are cousins, although Zuleika has grown up thinking that he is her brother; in the exotic setting of idealised eastern love and hatred, savage but beautiful weapons and 'fragrant beads of amber', there is no room for the expression of conventional views on incestuous love. Large numbers of readers were content to ignore such issues and to share the intoxication of those who, hearing the supernatural unseen bird in the graveyard at the end of the poem

> *cannot leave*
> *The spot, but linger there and grieve,*
> *As if they loved in vain.*

The Bride of Abydos sold six thousand copies in a month.

For all its sentimentality *The Bride*, like *The Giaour* and the other popular oriental tales which follow, also has a political dimension. In these poems traditional repressive authority is opposed to the actual or desired freedom of youth, lovers, pirates and females. This had particular resonance in a society where freedom of speech and assembly were often prevented and where many people associated libertarianism and individualism with revolutionary and Napoleonic France. Yet the fantasy setting of the tales enabled many conservative readers to enjoy them without having to compromise their principles. Similarly, the tales could be read as personal utterances by either the author or at least a recognisably Byronic figure, but readers were unlikely to suspect that extreme love in the exotic east actually reflected incest in the seemingly prosaic west. Few people, perhaps, seriously believed the rumour

George Gordon, Lord Byron

Byron in 1815, the year of his marriage and Napoleon's defeat at Waterloo, in an engraving after James Holmes.

National Portrait Gallery

that Byron, during his eastern travels, had actually become a pirate-chief like his Conrad who, cruel to all but his beloved Medora, 'left a Corsair's name to other times,/Link'd with one virtue, and a thousand crimes'. Equally, and fortunately, few people commented when Augusta Leigh gave her daughter, born on 15 April 1814, the names Elizabeth Medora; Byron seems very likely to have been the father.)

Conrad and Medora appear in *The Corsair*, written in ten days in December 1813 and published on 1 February 1814. The new tale excited such expectation that it sold ten thousand copies on the day of publication ('a thing perfectly unprecedented', Murray was delighted to report). Dallas was again the fortunate possessor of the copyright. (At last in August Byron himself accepted Murray's £700 for the copyright of *Lara*, the sequel to *The Corsair*.)

Byron was now at the height of his fame. There was not only a Byronic hero – and in the later tales, increasingly, a more dynamic heroine – but a Byronic look: pale, refined, open-necked, with at least a hint of suffering. The suffering became more unequivocal and the public perception less uncritical when, after years of wondering whether to go abroad again (perhaps permanently) or to marry, he chose the latter.

The hope of increased funds played some part in his decision, although Annabella Milbanke was potentially rather than actually rich – she was next in line to her mother as heir of her ailing uncle Lord Wentworth. More important however, as Augusta Leigh herself insisted, was the need to put an end to the dangerous incestuous affair and especially the possibility of its becoming common knowledge. So, while considering other candidates, Byron renewed the 'Annabella scheme'. Her letters made clear her continuing interest.

From the outset it ought to have been obvious that the two were mismatched. She had doubts about his morals and his loose attitude to religion. (He supposed he believed in God, he told her, but had never found religion helpful.) He diagnosed for Lady Melbourne her niece's 'awkward kind of correctness – with a dependence upon her own infallibility which will or may lead her into some egregious blunder'. Milbanke believed, essentially, that she would be able to improve or reform Byron. But his second, accepted proposal (September 1814) came nine months after they had last met and this separation helped the pair to delude themselves that the marriage could work. When, after delaying as long as possible, Byron at last arrived at Seaham in

Durham to visit the Milbankes in November 1814, there was some uncomfortableness between them. ('She seems to have more feeling than we imagined,' he wrote to the trusty Lady Melbourne, 'but is the most *silent* woman I ever encountered – which perplexes me extremely'.)

Whatever doubts there had been on either side, the wedding took place in the drawing-room at Seaham on the morning of 2 January 1815. Hobhouse, who was best man, recorded that during the ceremony the bride

> *was as firm as a rock ... and looked steadily at Byron. She repeated the words
> audibly and well. Byron hitched at first when he said, 'I, George Gordon', and
> when he came to 'With all my worldly goods I thee endow', looked at me with
> a half-smile. ... She came in her travelling-dress soon after; a slate-coloured
> satin pelisse trimmed with white fur, and sat quietly in the drawing-room.
> Byron was calm and as usual. I felt as if I had buried a friend.*

Tensions continued to be apparent during the honeymoon at Halnaby Hall in Yorkshire, although there were clearly more moments of happiness than Lady Byron later chose to remember. Deeper problems began to be apparent when the couple visited Augusta Leigh on their way south to London. The siblings' shared jokes and evident affection for each other may not yet have led Annabella to suspect the true nature of their relationship but it was certainly enough to make her feel excluded. (Augusta, however, tried throughout the marriage to help Annabella.) Besides, there were likely to be difficulties between the prim, inexperienced young lady and the libertine, ironical, troubled, travelled, perhaps most famous Englishman of the day. (Wellington had to defeat Napoleon at Waterloo later in the year in order, for a time, to take over this role.) There were interludes of mutual affection but as the year went on Byron was increasingly given to sarcasm, heavy drinking, and occasional unnerving pistol-brandishing. He also boasted about the affair he was having with an actress, Susan Boyce. Understandably, Annabella found it difficult to cope with his mood swings and provocative comments. He felt she should take what he said less seriously.

On 10 December 1815 the Byrons' daughter, Augusta Ada – always known as Ada – was born. Byron was evidently fond of the child – fonder, his wife observed, than of her. Money problems contributed to Byron's blacker moods. Newstead was still unsold and bailiffs occupied the London house for a time not long before Ada's birth; he was still refusing princely sums offered by his publisher. Lady Byron was now coming to the conclusion that her husband might actually be insane and went on seeking legal and medical advice in this connection after leaving London with her child on 15 January 1816. On 2 February Byron was surprised to receive a letter from his father-in-law proposing that the couple separate. For some weeks he professed his mystification, continuing love, and desire for a reconciliation, but Lady Byron, although at times in an agony of regret, became increasingly implacable. She was encouraged by her parents and legal representatives not to see her husband. Caroline Lamb helpfully told her about his homosexual liaisons. Hobhouse found his friend 'a prey to the alternate passions of pity, regret, love, and indignation'. By the end of February it was fairly clear that the separation would be permanent. (It became official in April.) In March he sent Annabella his poem 'Fare Thee Well', part lament, part accusation:

Though my many faults defaced me,

Could no other arm be found,

Than the one which once embraced me

To inflict a cureless wound?

Meanwhile, seemingly unaffected by his private problems, Byron's literary life had continued through 1815. He wrote the eastern tales *The Siege of Corinth* and *Parisina* and published *Hebrew Melodies*, which includes the lyric, inspired by the sight of his cousin Anne Wilmot at a London party in 1814,

She walks in beauty, like the night

Of cloudless climes and starry skies

And all that's best of dark and bright

Meet in her aspect and her eyes ...

He became a member of the management sub-committee at the newly rebuilt Drury Lane Theatre. He met and became the good friend of the writer Walter Scott. He gave money to Coleridge – another former (and in this case future) target of his satire – and helped him to place *Christabel* with his own publisher, Murray. When the scandal of the separation broke, complete with rumours of 'unnatural practices', Byron was ostracised by much of London society and found it easiest to depart – as he had long intended – for self-imposed exile on the other side of the English Channel. (Debts were another major factor). He remained a notorious but fascinating figure; 'Don't look at him, he is dangerous to look at,' the respectable Lady Liddell admonished her daughter on seeing the wicked lord in Rome in 1817.

⫷ *Waterloo, Switzerland, Childe Harold III*

Byron's exile was the outer sign of his need to re-define himself after his fall from the pinnacle of social success. In his work too there was an opportunity for re-definition. Near the beginning of *Childe Harold* canto three he reflects on the reason for and process of his writing:

> *'Tis to create, and in creating live*
> *A being more intense, that we endow*
> *With form our fancy, gaining as we give*
> *The life we image, even as I do now.*

Having lost London and Augusta the author was more willing than usual to countenance poetry as a way of living more intensely. At once arguing the point and demonstrating the experience ('even as I do now'), he captures something of the very moment of writing – as he did more often in his letters, diaries, and late poetry.

Wandering again like 'Self-exiled Harold' he continued *Childe Harold's Pilgrimage* into this third canto, probing his changed perception of the world since 1812

> *With nought of hope left, but with less of gloom;*
> *The very knowledge that he lived in vain,*
> *That all was over on this side the tomb,*
> *Had made Despair a smilingness assume.*

The despair and the smilingness of the first months of exile are both present when he writes to his sister from Geneva on 8 September that 'the Separation – has broken my heart – I feel as if an Elephant had trodden on it'. The sense of things ending – 'all was over on this side the tomb' – leads Harold naturally to the field of Waterloo, which Byron visited on 4 May 1816 and where less than a year earlier Napoleon Bonaparte had met his final defeat.

Byron had mixed feelings about Napoleon. In youth he had responded to the political appeal of this energetic heir of the French Revolution and enemy of European monarchies. (The appeal was less apparent to the generation born in the 1770s – Wordsworth, Coleridge, Beethoven – who had witnessed as adults the swift move from republicanism to absolutism: when Napoleon became Emperor in 1804 Beethoven erased the dedication to him of the Eroica symphony.) Napoleon also figured in European minds as a kind of Byronic hero, strong, lone, absolute, perhaps satanic. Byron, who in his hour of fame was esteemed 'The grand Napoleon of the realms of rhyme' (*Don Juan*, canto eleven), clearly identified with him, envied his achievements in the realm of deeds rather than rhyme, and was aware that they each had recently gone down to defeat and exile. The capacious coach in which Byron travelled was modelled on Napoleon's. (It cost £500, had to be shipped rapidly before the bailiffs could seize it, and was never paid for.) By now he was far from uncritical; 'Ode to Napoleon Buonaparte' reflects with bitter irony on his ignominious and ignoble survival after abdicating at Fontainebleau in 1814. But Byron was at least equally dissatisfied with the restoration of the Bourbon monarchy. He had been delighted when the emperor escaped from Elba, landed near Antibes, and to general astonishment entered Paris, in March 1815. Then Byron told Thomas Moore

The opening of Byron's 'Ode to Napoleon Buonaparte', a meditation on the fall of the emperor in 1814.

The British Library 11644.n.27

ODE

TO

NAPOLEON BUONAPARTE.

I.

'Tis done—but yesterday a King !
And arm'd with Kings to strive—
And now thou art a nameless thing
So abject — yet alive !
Is this the man of thousand thrones,
Who strew'd our Earth with hostile bones,
And can he thus survive ?
Since he, miscall'd the Morning Star,
Nor man nor fiend hath fall'n so far.

It is impossible not to be dazzled and overwhelmed by his character and career. Nothing ever so disappointed me as his abdication, and nothing could have reconciled me to him but some such revival as his recent exploit; though no one could anticipate such a complete and brilliant renovation.

Claire Clairmont (1798-1879), in a painting by Aemelia Curran. After the deaths of her daughter Allegra, P.B. Shelley, and Byron, she worked as a governess in Austria and Russia. In old age she lived in Florence, a survivor from the distant past. Her story was the initial inspiration for Henry James' The Aspern Papers (1888).

Newstead Abbey

Soon, however, Waterloo was lost and Bonaparte consigned to St Helena and history. Pondering on the field of battle where thousands died, among them Byron's cousin Frederick Howard, it was difficult to subscribe to the Napoleonic myth. And yet – partly perhaps because of the old self-identification – the flawed and fallen emperor remained a subject of fascination: one whose spirit was 'antithetically mixt', mighty and petty, 'Extreme in all things!', one who overreached himself because 'quiet to quick bosoms is a hell'.

Among the various manuscripts of *Childe Harold's Pilgrimage* canto three are two fair copies made in Switzerland in the summer of 1816, one begun by Byron but largely in the hand of Mary Wollstonecraft Godwin, the other, later used as printer's copy, by Claire Clairmont. These step-sisters and their companion Percy Bysshe Shelley – co-habiting with and soon to marry Mary – were of great importance in Byron's life over the next six years. The young women – both eighteen when they came to Switzerland – grew up in the radical, intellectual London household of William Godwin, novelist, educator, and reformer; his first wife, the pioneer feminist Mary Wollstonecraft, had died soon after giving birth to Mary. Shelley, poet, radical thinker, vegetarian, atheist, appealed to Mary Godwin for his ideas as well as his person. In 1814, accompanied by Claire Clairmont, William Godwin's stepdaughter, the couple ran away to France on their first foreign expedition. However differently Byron might have reacted to such earnest, unconventional people in the years of London success, he was happy to seek their company now, although in some ways he would have preferred Clairmont to be absent. A few weeks before he had left England she had introduced herself to him by letter and persuaded him to have sex with her – 'if a girl of eighteen comes prancing to you at all hours – there is but one way' he later told his banker Douglas Kinnaird. He was already tiring of her but, he claimed in a letter to Augusta, found it difficult 'to play the Stoic with a woman who had scrambled eight hundred miles to unphilosophize me'.

From June 1816 the Shelley group was established in a small house by Lake Geneva at Montalègre. Byron, close by at Villa Diodati with a fine view of the lake and mountains, spent increasing amounts of time in their company, although, disliking the idea of intellectual women, he was interested above all in Shelley. Shelley, with none of Byron's cynicism and world-weariness, had inalienable convictions about the need and the possibility of bettering humankind and about the power of poetry to act as 'the trumpet of a prophecy' ('Ode to the West Wind', 1819). As they talked at length at Villa Diodati or while sailing on the lake in the small boat they had bought together, Byron came greatly to admire this sincere idealist although he remained doubtful about some of the ideals. As he remembered it later in conversation with Shelley's cousin Thomas Medwin, the young enthusiast 'used to dose me with Wordsworth physic even to nausea'. In the powerful visual setting of Lake Geneva, Byron, much in need of nature's healing power, was able at times to accept the pantheism of Wordsworth, and Shelley's atheistic but no less rapt version of it. Its influence can be seen in places in *Childe Harold* canto three, parts of which were written or revised at this time: much as in Wordsworth's 'Tintern Abbey' 'High mountains are a feeling, but the hum/ Of human cities torture'; the soul can flee from fleshly creatures 'And with the sky, the peak, the heaving plain/Of ocean, or the stars, mingle, and not in vain'. The canto, however, soon returns with some relief to 'that which is immediate'. Byron remained painfully aware of the difficulty of mingling with sky and peak; in September, when he toured the Bernese Oberland, he told his sister that no amount of avalanche, mountain, glacier, forest, cloud have 'for one moment – lightened the weight upon my heart – nor enabled me to lose my own wretched identity in the majesty and the power and the glory – around – above – and beneath me'.

At the end of June the two poets spent a week sailing around the lake. Shelley described 'the mighty forests ... and lawns of exquisite verdure, and mountains with bare and icy points'. At the castle of Chillon they contemplated the grim dungeons and heard the story of François Bonivard, a sixteenth-century political prisoner confined there for six years by the Duke of Savoy. A few days later, possibly when rain detained them at Ouchy, Byron wrote 'The Prisoner of Chillon', a monologue spoken by Bonivard remembering the dark prison vault beneath the level of the lake (as

Of l'n delirious with its dead
But there were horrors — this was woe
Unmixed with such — but sure & slow
He faded — and so calm & meek —
So softly worn — so sweetly weak, —
So tearless — yet so tender; kind
And grieved for those he left behind
With all the while a cheek whose bloom
Was as a mockery of the tomb —
Whose tints as gently sunk away
As a departing rainbow's ray —
An eye of most transparent light
That almost made the dungeon bright
And not a word of murmur — not
A groan o'er his untimely lot —
A little talk of better days —
A little hope my own to raise.
For I was sunk in silence — lost
In this last loss of all the most
And then the sighs he would suppress

Mary Wollstonecraft Godwin's transcript of Byron's 'The Prisoner of Chillon', with revisions by Byron.

The British Library, Scrope Davies Papers, Loan 70, vol. VII f.6v.

Byron mistakenly supposed it once had been), the death of his captive brothers, a tantalising glimpse of mountain, lake, green isle and eagle. At last, inured to chains, friend of the spiders and the mice, 'even I/Regain'd my freedom with a sigh'.

On the evenings of incessant rain which preceded this tour of the lake the whole group, including the young doctor who was travelling with Byron, John William Polidori, would gather by the fireside at Villa Diodati. 'Many and long', recalled Mary Shelley in 1831, 'were the conversations between Lord Byron and Shelley, to which I was a devout but nearly silent listener'. They talked, amongst much else, about 'the nature of the principle of life'; 'Perhaps a corpse would be re-animated; ... perhaps the component parts of a creature might be manufactured, brought together, and endued with vital warmth'. They also read tales of horror together, and Byron plunged Shelley, who was prone to hallucinations, into a virtual fit by declaiming, after midnight, the description from Coleridge's *Christabel* of Geraldine's 'bosom and half her side – /Hideous, deformed, and pale of hue'. The group had resolved each to write their own ghost story. Most of the efforts were abortive. Byron wrote a few pages which later inspired Polidori's *The Vampyre*, widely received as Byron's own. But it was the eighteen-year-old Mary Godwin who, amid talk of re-animation and ghosts and vampires, came upon a famous idea for a story when 'night waned upon this talk' and she 'saw with shut eyes, but acute mental vision ... the pale student of unhallowed arts kneeling beside the thing he had put together' and the thing 'on the working of some powerful engine, show signs of life'. *Frankenstein* was begun.

'The illustrious poets' were 'annoyed by the platitude of prose', as the preface to *Frankenstein* modestly puts it, and 'speedily relinquished their uncongenial task'. Shelley in fact, feeling overshadowed or blocked by Byron, wrote little in any form at this time. The Shelley party, including a sad, pregnant Clairmont, left for England at the end of August bearing the canto three and 'Prisoner of Chillon' manuscripts for delivery to Murray. Meanwhile Byron, productive as ever, had begun work on *Manfred, a Dramatic Poem* (completed in Italy in 1817). Like the evening conversations at Diodati, *Manfred* explores the basis of life, but in a more 'wild – metaphysical – and inexplicable' manner (as he described it to Murray in February 1817) than *Frankenstein*. The setting in the Alps is largely that of the 'Alpine Journal' he kept during his Bernese tour with Hobhouse in September 1816 after the departure of the Shelleys. 'The hero', continues Byron's letter to Murray, is

> *a kind of magician tormented by a species of remorse – the cause of which is left half unexplained. ... He at last goes to the very abode of the Evil principle in propria persona – to evocate a ghost – which appears – and gives him an ambiguous and disagreeable answer – and in the 3d. act he is found by his attendants dying in a tower – where he studied his art.*

Manfred, the magician who can invoke and control spirits (a variation, as Goethe himself realised, on Faust and his pact with the Devil) had loved Astarte. She, as readers were now only too eager to observe, was his sister. But *Manfred* is rather more complex, experimental and exciting than this autobiographical sidelight may suggest. It sold poorly and suffers in places from too much of the pseudo-Elizabethan language used by poets of the period when writing plays or dramatic poems, but its impassioned scenes of Jungfrau-top incantation, meeting of mortal and spirit, living and dead, holy abbot and diabolical spirits, commended it not only to some readers but also to composers and painters including Robert Schumann and John Martin.

'Manfred on the Jungfrau', a watercolour of 1837 by John Martin. When Manfred is about to spring from the cliff, the Chamois Hunter 'seizes and retains him with a sudden grasp'.

Birmingham Museums and Art Gallery

61

❧ *Venice*

The heavy Napoleonic coach, with Byron, Hobhouse, servants and couriers all armed to the teeth in the expectation of encountering bandits, now rumbled into Italy. Byron was deeply read in Italian history and literature, already spoke the language fairly fluently, and was eager to see places connected with the great poets. He was also interested in such historical figures as Lucrezia Borgia, the cultured, attractive Renaissance Duchess of Ferrara, member of a sinister and murderous papal family. He purloined a single strand of her golden hair – trophy of an otherwise unattainable woman – from the Ambrosian Library in Milan. Italy engaged Byron also in more personal terms: after the marriage débâcle he could feel, near the traces of ancient glory, like 'a ruin amidst ruins', and he evidently identified his own ostracism with the way Italy had treated *its* poets. Dante had been exiled from Florence, Boccaccio condemned for his allegedly immoral tales, and the passionate, idealistic Torquato Tasso imprisoned as a madman in a cavernous dungeon in Ferrara. (Annabella, Byron might have said, had a similar fate in mind for him.) In political terms, too, Italy engaged him: Tasso was locked up chiefly, legend had it, for presuming to love Leonora, sister of the Duke, and thus his plight could stand for that of an Italy tyrannised by its Austrian, papal, and Bourbon overlords; the nascent hopes for a new Italy – the first stirrings of the *risorgimento* movement which eventually delivered a unified Italy in the 1860s – could be espoused more readily and less controversially than practical support for Byron's native frame-breakers. Tasso features both in *Childe Harold's Pilgrimage* canto four and in *The Lament of Tasso*, 1817.

Venice, Byron's principal destination, had 'always been (next to the east)', he told Thomas Moore, 'the greenest island of my imagination'. It catered to his politics, his love of history, and his periodic love of dissipation. The Venice section of the fourth canto of *Childe Harold*, written in the summer of 1817, combines the history, the politics, Byron's delight in water (physically consummated in his $3\frac{3}{4}$ mile swim from Lido across the Lagoon and up the Grand Canal), and the vein of melancholy often present in the earlier cantos:

I stood in Venice on the Bridge of Sighs;

A palace and a prison on each hand:

I saw from out the wave her structures rise

As from the stroke of the enchanter's wand:

A thousand years their cloudy wings expand

Around me, and a dying Glory smiles

O'er the far times, when many a subject land

Look'd to the winged Lion's marble piles,

Where Venice sat in state, thron'd on her

hundred isles!

The Bridge of Sighs, an engraving in Thirty Illustrations of Childe Harold, *1855. 'Everything about Venice is, or was, extraordinary – her aspect is like a dream, and her history is like a romance' (Byron's preface to* Marino Faliero, *1821).*

The British Library 7868.d.15

The thousand-year independent Venetian republic had ended at last when the city capitulated to Napoleon in 1797. Signs of the republic were still to be seen in the magnificence of St Mark's Basilica, before which 'still glow' the 'steeds of brass', the Doges' palace and prison, the decaying remains of the last state barge or Bucentaur. There was, at this time, no immediate prospect of reviving the power which had once underwritten the glory. Byron's engagement with the politics of Venice was confined to 'the far times' and such works as *Marino Faliero*, 1821, a verse drama inspired by the foiled conspiracy of a medieval Doge, in league with poorer citizens, to overthrow his fellow patricians.

More immediately, Byron took energetic advantage of the southern freedom from constraint. His first main affair was with Marianna Segati, the wife of ' "a Merchant of Venice" [a draper], who is a good deal occupied with business' and in whose house in the narrow Frezzeria, near Piazza San Marco, Byron lodged in 1816-17. In appearance, he told Moore, she was 'altogether like an antelope. She has the large, black, oriental eyes, with that peculiar expression in them which is seen rarely among Europeans – even the Italians'. The overwhelming visual delight most people still experience on first encountering the buildings, waters and skies of Venice extended for Byron to the inhabitants. And the delight was not only visual and sexual: he enjoyed the dialect, met Venetians from countesses to gondoliers on intimate terms, and regularly visited the Armenian monks on the island of San Lazzaro for lessons in their language – 'something craggy' for the mind 'to break upon'. He saw at close quarters the passionate behaviour more often repressed in colder England. The 'antelope' Segati was fierce enough to seize her sister-in-law by the hair when she showed an interest in Byron and bestow upon her 'some sixteen slaps, which would have made your ear ache only to hear their echo' before falling into a fit in his arms.

Villa Foscarini, La Mira. Byron told Hobhouse, in a letter of June 1817, that this 'abode ... is well enough – with more space than splendour – and not much of that'. It was also too near the road; Venetians on the mainland 'seem to think they never can have dust enough to compensate for their long immersion'.

The British Library 10862.c.5

Dramatic behaviour was even more the forte of Margarita Cogni, whom he met in the summer of 1817 while riding near Villa Foscarini, the house he leased for six months at La Mira on the Brenta. (The banks of the canal were the traditional summer retreat of the Venetian nobility, and are still lined with fine palaces. Villa Foscarini, however, later became a post office.) A *fornarina*, or baker's wife, she attracted him by her sheer confidence as well as her looks. She became his housekeeper at Palazzo Mocenigo, the sprawling house on the Grand Canal which he leased in 1818 and 1819 and filled with fourteen servants and a menagerie of monkeys, a fox, and mastiffs. Here she knocked down her rivals amid 'great confusion – and demolition of head dresses and handkerchiefs'; 'she was the terror of men, women and children, for she had the strength of an Amazon with the temper of Medea. She was a fine animal – but quite untameable', Byron claimed to Murray after Margarita had – following failed attempts to knife him and to drown herself in the canal – finally accepted that their liaison was over.

A principal joy of Venice was the Carnival, when, as Byron puts it in *Beppo*, 1818,

The people take their fill of recreation,
And buy repentance, ere they grow devout,
However high their rank, or low their station,
With fiddling, feasting, dancing, drinking, masking,
And other things which may be had for asking.

Byron indulged to the full in this hedonistic release from northern propriety, and by the time Carnival gave way to Lent 'with all its abstinence and Sacred Music' he confessed to Moore that even he was becoming somewhat jaded and uttered for his friend some appropriate sentiments in verse:

> *So we'll go no more a roving*
> *So late into the night,*
> *Though the heart be still as loving,*
> *And the moon be still as bright.*
>
> *For the sword outwears its sheath,*
> *And the soul wears out the breast,*
> *And the heart must pause to breathe,*
> *And Love itself have rest.*
>
> *Though the night was made for loving,*
> *And the day returns too soon,*
> *Yet we'll go no more a roving*
> *By the light of the moon.*

But in *Beppo* (written rapidly in October 1817) the spirit of 'roving' survived. The role reversals and masquerades, licensed anarchy and sexual freedom of carnival are the essence of this deliberately digressive story of a Venetian woman who lives with her lover (or 'vice-husband') during the prolonged absence of her spouse; all three come to an easy accommodation when the husband ('a merchant trading to Aleppo,/His name Giuseppe, call'd more briefly, Beppo') unexpectedly reappears. The narrator, as in many a masked meeting, does not know the woman's real name; he calls her Laura – fun at the expense of Petrarch's unobtainable beloved. The style and manner of the poem, too, add to the carnival atmosphere. Here at last the casual tone of the letters enters Byron's poetry: intelligent, wickedly witty, liable to self-mockery or to poking fun at the reader, completely in control yet seemingly spontaneous. At the fifty-second verse, still about to start telling Laura's story, the

Laura in Beppo. *'The women only thought it quite amazing/That, at her time of life, so many were/Admirers still, - but/"Men are so debased, Those brazen creatures always suit their taste."'*

The British Library 789.f.30

narrator declares 'I've half a mind to tumble down to prose,/But verse is more in fashion – so here goes'. The unexpected rhyme – another irresistible example leaves 'upon her sad knee' 'this Adriatic Ariadne' – like much else in *Beppo* will be a familiar feature of Byron's greatest work, *Don Juan*. As there, the humour often has a serious purpose; conversational asides, like comic rhymes, can question conventions, puncture hypocrisies, drop in the truth – when Laura's husband sails away ''Tis said that their last parting was pathetic,/As partings often are, or ought to be'.

Apparently Byron himself changed styles. Thomas Moore, seeing him at La Mira and Venice in 1819 for the first time in five years, later recalled that he

Byron's first version of Childe Harold, *IV.103-4, written in July 1817. Stanza 103 is part of the meditation at the tomb of Cecilia Metella, beginning 'Perchance she died in age – surviving all – Charms – kindred – children – with the silver gray/ On her long tresses.'*

John Murray

found him 'fatter both in person and face', bewhiskered and with a coat and cap of 'rather foreign air'. 'He was still, however, eminently handsome: and, in exchange for whatever his features might have lost of their high, romantic character, they had become more fitted for the expression of' his 'arch, waggish wisdom' or 'Epicurean play of humour'. The fourth canto of *Childe Harold*, sent home to Murray with Hobhouse in January 1818, was the last flowering of the 'high, romantic character' which had first won readers. After the meditation on Venice the poem moves on through Italy, as Byron did during his excursion in the spring of 1817, to Rome. Here he stayed at 66 Piazza di Spagna, opposite the house where John Keats would die in February 1821. (Byron on a number of occasions spoke scornfully of Keats' poetry, although he was moved to some compassion by Shelley's elegy on him, *Adonais* – in spite of 'all the fantastic fopperies of his style', Byron wrote to Murray, Keats' 'genius ... was undoubtedly of great promise'.) He was 'delighted with Rome'; 'it is a fine thing to see. ... As a *whole – ancient and modern –* it beats Greece – Constantinople – every thing – at least that I have ever seen'. As edited by memory the city became, in the *Childe Harold* canto, a repository of images of time, its mysteries, casualties and survivors, centred on such monuments as the 'stern round tower of other days' on the Appian Way: the tomb of a woman who may have been old or young, 'inveterate in virtue' or 'Profuse of joy', but about whom all that is actually known is that Cecilia Metella 'died,/The wealthiest Roman's wife; Behold his love or pride!'. Ruins also, once more, have personal associations for the poet. In the moonlit Colosseum, 'This long-explored but still exhaustless mine/Of contemplation', thoughts on time lead to thoughts of revenge – on nameless foes who

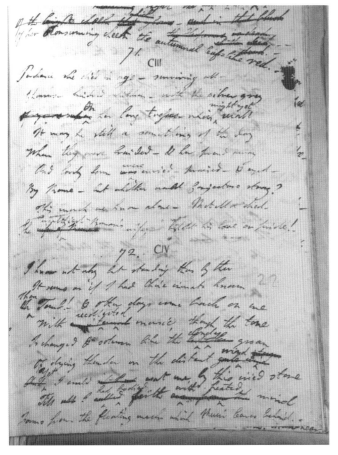

evidently include Lady Byron, her family and supporters and Caroline Lamb – and then of forgiveness, although one which may amount to a form of vengeance: his 'curse shall be Forgiveness' and when he expires

> *Something unearthly, which they dream not of,*
> *Like the remembered tone of a mute lyre,*
> *Shall on their softened spirits sink, and move*
> *In hearts all rocky now the late remorse of love.*

Claire Clairmont had better reasons for self-pity. Her child by Byron, Clara Allegra, had been born at Bath in January 1817. He did not regard her or the Shelleys as fit people to bring up his daughter; in spite of his own scepticism about organized religion he wished her to receive traditional religious training, safe from such 'free-thinkers'. He therefore exercised his legal right to custody. He greatly liked Shelley

Byron at Palazzo Mocenigo, on the Grand Canal in Venice, where Byron lived in 1818 and 1819. Lithograph after John Scarlett Davies.

Newstead Abbey

himself, however, and was prepared to communicate with Clairmont only through him. After the separation of mother and child in April 1818 Allegra lived variously at Palazzo Mocenigo, at the house in Venice of the British consul Richard Belgrave Hoppner and his wife Isabella, and finally from March 1821 at a convent in Bagnacavallo, near Ravenna.

On 22 August 1818 Shelley and Claire Clairmont, who was desperately anxious about Allegra, arrived in Venice. Since it was clear that her presence at Palazzo Mocenigo would be counter-productive, Shelley went alone, leaving her with the Hoppners and Allegra but telling Byron that his womenfolk were in Padua. (Mary Shelley was in fact still at Bagni di Lucca, some five days' journey away, with her children.) Byron was delighted to see Shelley again, and, to his considerable surprise, suggested that the whole Shelley party – and Allegra – should move into the villa he had leased in the Euganean hills at Este. (Byron himself, avoiding Claire, would remain in Venice.) Soon, they were talking of other matters, including poetry (Byron recited parts of the new *Childe Harold* canto) and religion. They talked from 3.00 p.m. until 5.00 a.m., moving from palace to gondola to riding on the Lido, at this time 'a bare strand/Of hillocks, heaped from ever-shifting sand,/Matted with thistles and amphibious weeds' (Shelley's *Julian and Maddalo*), and back to the palace. The poets met again in subsequent weeks; in the meantime, largely to prevent Byron from finding out that he had been lied to about the whereabouts of Mary and Claire, Shelley told his wife to bring the children as fast as possible to Este. Their daughter Clara, who was already feverish when she set off, died almost certainly as a result of the hot and hectic journey.

The poets' long August conversation was the main source of Shelley's poem *Julian and Maddalo*, an account both of their fascination for each other and of their fundamentally different philosophies. Julian's optimism about the possibility of human betterment is opposed to Maddalo's Byronic scepticism:

> *We descanted, and I (for ever still*
> *Is it not wise to make the best of ill?)*
> *Argued against despondency, but pride*
> *Made my companion take the darker side.*

But the poem – like the conversations – remains aware of both points of view, and aware that Maddalo's or Byron's 'more serious conversation is a sort of intoxication; men are held by it as a spell'; the Shelleyan idealist acknowledges that just possibly, as Maddalo pithily observes, 'You talk Utopia'.

Privately, Shelley thought Byron's philosophical 'despondency' was the result of self-disgust at his life among 'the lowest sort' of the ignorant and filthy women of Venice; 'contemplating in the distorted mirror of his own thoughts, the nature and the destiny of man, what can he behold but objects of contempt and despair?' But Shelley still hoped to change his friend, to somehow release the potential of this 'person of the most consummate genius, and capable, if he would direct his energies to such an end, of becoming the redeemer of his degraded country'. Optimism for the future combines with a statement of the power of human innocence in the brief appearance in *Julian and Maddalo* of a beautiful child evidently inspired by Allegra. At the end of the poem she reappears, grown up 'a wonder of this earth'. But, as if to confute Shelley's optimism, the real Allegra did not become a woman. She died of typhoid, aged five, at the convent in April 1822. Byron mourned her for a time and arranged for her to be buried in Harrow churchyard, as if to identify her with his own childhood. In his way he had cared for her, to some extent using her as a substitute for his legitimate daughter, Ada. But his grief was of course as nothing compared with that of Claire Clairmont, who lived on until 1879 with no kind memory of the man who had fathered her only child.

New directions: the first cantos of Don Juan, Teresa Guiccioli, Ravenna

In the summer of 1818 at Palazzo Mocenigo, Byron embarked, he told Moore, on 'a poem in the style and manner of "Beppo", encouraged by the success of the same. It is called "Don Juan", and it is meant to be a little quietly facetious upon every thing'. *Don Juan* occupied much of his energy between then and his departure for Greece in 1823. It tells, in sixteen cantos and the unfinished fragment of a seventeenth, the tale of Don Juan – a figure derived from the archetypal seducer of Spanish tradition whose most famous incarnation is Mozart's Don Giovanni. Byron's Don Juan – pronounced 'Jooan', capable of rhyming with, variously, 'ruin', 'brewing' and 'new one' – is a much less rapacious or methodical lover than the usual figure. In this work, which often parodies or alludes to the epic poems of Homer, Virgil and Milton, contrasting their certainties with modern uncertainties and hypocrisies, Juan is a hero only because no better candidates are available. (The first canto begins 'I want a hero: an uncommon want,/When every year and month sends forth a new one'.) Love on the whole simply comes upon him, and the poem too proceeds ostensibly without a plan: 'Sometimes with and sometimes without occasion,/I write what's uppermost, without delay'. More conventional heroes, poems and authors do not behave in such an apparently undisciplined fashion; neither, suggests Byron, does life.

As was the case with *Beppo*, the main sources for the 'style and manner' include John Hookham Frere's wittily digressive poem *Whistlecraft*, which Byron read in the autumn of 1817. Frere and Byron were also influenced by the mock-heroic verse of Luigi Pulci (1432-84) and later Italian poets. (Among prose writers the clearest general influence is that of the eighteenth-century English novelist Henry Fielding, and especially the digressive narrator and sympathetically fallible hero of *Tom Jones*.) In turning to these comic traditions he sought an antidote to the 'wrong revolutionary poetical system – or systems' which, he told Murray in September 1817, he and all other recent poets had been following. The achievement of 'us youth' is insignificant compared with that of Pope a century before. In *Don Juan*, as in *English Bards* at the beginning of Byron's career, a good approximation to Pope's sharp satire is sometimes achieved, but on the whole the note is more distinctive: neither Augustan nor Romantic. Byron is more digressive and self-referential than either Pope or Wordsworth, mocks himself, mocks the reader. Another distinctive feature, again as in *Beppo*, is the use of *ottava rima*, the rhyme-scheme used by Pulci and his successors. The pattern of rhymes – abababcc – is usually considered too difficult for English, where there are fewer rhyme-words. A stanza from the first canto should give a flavour of *Don Juan* more generally:

> *He thought about himself, and the whole earth,*
> *Of man the wonderful, and of the stars,*
> *And how the deuce they ever could have birth;*
> *And then he thought of earthquakes, and of wars,*
> *How many miles the moon might have in girth,*
> *Of air-balloons, and of the many bars*
> *To perfect knowledge of the boundless skies;*
> *And then he thought of Donna Julia's eyes.*

This stanza suggests the scale of serious epic; at the same time, we know from the previous stanza, it makes fun of Coleridge's metaphysical wonderings. The six lines of alternating rhymes give a sense of unfinalised wondering or epic possibilities while the final couplet moves rapidly to assert the point on which *Don Juan* so often insists, that physical desires and imperatives, this world now, more often govern life than the wonderful, the stars, or the finer points of philosophical enquiry. (Coleridge has taken to 'Explaining metaphysics to the nation –/I wish he would explain his Explanation', says Byron earlier.) The attraction between Juan and Julia moves towards its inevitable consummation, while the reader is equally aware of the narrator's voice and attitude – 'how the deuce ...'

Byron's letter to Moore on the first canto goes on to suggest that it may be 'too free for these very modest [i.e. prudish] times'. This was, as Byron was well aware, an understatement: there was predictable outrage from his once devoted

English audience that the very poet who had once celebrated constant love in such works as *The Corsair* should now chronicle a series of extra-marital adventures with understanding, even approval. Even the well known courtesan Harriette Wilson wrote, on reading the first two cantos of *Don Juan*, published in July 1819, to beg 'Dear *Adorable* Lord Byron, *don't* make a mere *coarse* old libertine of yourself'. Certainly he was willing to shock some readers and titillate others, but his more important avowed aim is to expose hypocrisy – the hypocrisy of a society in which Donna Julia, for instance, trapped in a marriage of convenience with a man many years her senior, himself unfaithful, is punished for loving Juan. Contemporary poets, moralists and clergy, with their denial or condemnation of human sexuality, were similarly open to attack. (There is also a personal agenda – Juan's strict, pious, hypocritical mother Inez is obviously directed at Lady Byron, the unfair victim of one of her husband's most ingenious solutions to the insatiable demand of *ottava rima* for rhymes: 'But – Oh! ye lords of ladies intellectual,/Inform us truly, have they not hen-peck'd you all?' Even the wronged wife, on reading the poem, admitted that she sometimes could not help smiling at such 'quizzing'.)

Part of Byron's savage attack on Lord Castlereagh, British foreign secretary between 1812 and 1822, in stanza 14 of the dedication to Don Juan, *which remained unpublished until 1832. Castlereagh, says Byron, is 'Cobbling at manacles for all mankind - /A tinkering slavemaker who mends old chains.'*

British Library
Ashley MS A326

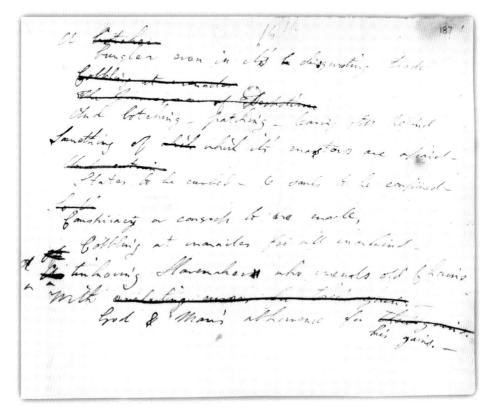

Political hypocrisy is also a target. Byron tells Moore that *Don Juan* 'is dedicated to Robert Southey in good, simple, savage verse' on his 'politics, and the way he got them'. (The dedication begins with the splendidly direct, sarcastic, and irreverent 'Bob Southey! You're a poet – poet Laureate,/And representative of all the race ...') Southey, once a champion of reform, has become the respectable, intolerant Tory laureate. Wordsworth and Coleridge figure similarly as turncoats, and foreign minister Castlereagh as enemy both of liberal reform in his native Ireland and of liberal causes in post-Napoleonic Europe. Byron's friends, who, with the notable exception of Shelley, urged him not to print this outrageous work, succeeded in persuading him to withdraw the dedication. Murray was afraid of prosecution for publishing subversive material and was, himself, besides, no liberal sympathiser (Jane Austen was one of his politically safer authors); nevertheless, in the hope of sales and with his once star author threatening to take his work elsewhere, he published the two cantos, without either Byron's name or his own, in July 1819.

Byron's authorship was, however, obvious. Condemnation was widespread. There were some obvious targets for reviewers: a parody of the Ten Commandments, for instance, beginning 'Thou shalt believe in Milton, Dryden, Pope;/ Thou shalt not set up Wordsworth, Coleridge, Southey', was not merely annoying to supporters of the 'Lake Poets' trio but, it could be claimed, blasphemous. It was the fate of Juan's tutor, Pedrillo, in canto two which gave the cue for indignation to an anonymous reviewer in *Blackwood's Magazine* in August 1819. Juan has been sent off to travel 'for four springs' with the tutor after being discovered in Julia's bedroom. (She meanwhile is consigned to a convent where,

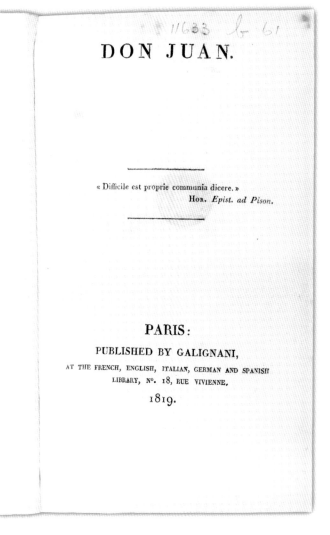

The title page of the unauthorised Galignani edition of Don Juan, *cantos one and two, 1819. Like the authorised edition published by John Murray, this one was published anonymously. Copyright restrictions began to be applied only later in the nineteenth century.*

The British Library 11633.b.61

DON JUAN.

« Difficile est proprie communia dicere. »
Hor. *Epist. ad Pison.*

PARIS:

PUBLISHED BY GALIGNANI,

AT THE FRENCH, ENGLISH, ITALIAN, GERMAN AND SPANISH LIBRARY, N°. 18, RUE VIVIENNE.

1819.

the poem acknowledges, she will go on loving Juan while he, for all his grief at parting, will soon forget her.) The ship founders in a storm and some of the passengers, including Juan and the comically cowardly Pedrillo, escape in a long-boat while the people and provisions aboard the cutter go down. The most fearful sound in the ears of the lost, *Blackwood's* submits, is 'the demoniacal laugh with which this unpitying brother [the poet] exults over the contemplation of despair. Will our readers believe that the most innocent of all his odious sarcasms is contained in these two lines? – "They grieved for those who perish'd with the cutter,/And also for the biscuit casks and butter".'

But in context this apparent flippancy of tone is in fact less sarcasm than a brave refusal to deny that frightened, starving people may think more of their stomachs than of their fellow mortals. Flippancy and gravity alternate and blend as they do in life. When 'The longings of the cannibal arise' and Pedrillo draws the fatal lot he dies with unexpected dignity; but, before we can ponder this for long, comic rhymes are reasserting the real hard-heartedness or resilience of survivors – and of readers who laugh when the uneatable parts of the tutor 'Regaled two sharks, who follow'd o'er the billow –/The sailors ate the rest of poor Pedrillo'. Again the tone shifts as – momentarily more gratifying to moralists – those who ate Pedrillo go 'raging mad', blaspheme, and die despairing. 'And if I laugh at any mortal thing', Byron will declare later in the poem, ''Tis that I may not weep'.

Another critic objected to 'the quick succession of fun and gravity' in *Don Juan*, declaring that 'we are never scorched and drenched at the same time'. This elicited from Byron, in a letter to Murray of 12 August 1819, a reply which itself aptly mingles humour and exasperation: 'Did he never play at cricket or walk a mile in hot weather? ... did he never swim in the sea at Noonday with the sun in his eyes and on his head – which all the foam of ocean could not cool. ... Was he ever in ... the sulphureous waves of hell? (where he ought to be for his "scorching and drenching at the same time")'.

In April 1819, the same month in which Byron despatched the finished version of canto two to Murray, he fell in love with Countess Teresa Guiccioli. He had first met her, briefly, in January 1818, a few days after her marriage, at the age of about eighteen, to the fifty-seven-year-old Count Alessandro Guiccioli. (She was

his third wife.) Her situation bore at least some resemblance to that of Julia in *Don Juan* canto one. Byron later explained her position to Thomas Medwin:

> *Do you know how a girl is brought up here? Almost from infancy she is deprived of the endearments of home, and shut up in a convent till she has attained a marriageable or marketable age. The father now looks out for a suitable son-in-law. ... His object is to find some needy man of equal rank, or a very rich one, the older the better, who will consent to take his daughter off his hands, under the market price. ... There is no love on either side. What happiness is to be expected, or constancy, from such a liaison? Is it not natural, that in her intercourse with a world, of which she knows and has seen nothing, and unrestrained mistress of her own time and actions, she should find somebody to like better, and who likes her better, than her husband?*

Within days Byron and Teresa Guiccioli had consummated their love. About a week later she and her husband returned home to Ravenna, and that might have been the end of yet another relationship. But Byron was tiring of the 'promiscuous concubinage' of his life in Venice. Everything there, he wrote to her on 25 April (in Italian – she knew no English), seemed monotonous now; for some years he had tried systematically 'to avoid strong passions, having suffered too much from the tyranny of love', to enjoy himself without attaching importance to the enjoyment, to remain indifferent. But now she has put to flight all his resolutions and he will 'become what you wish – perhaps happy in your love, but never again at peace'. He was drawn to her both physically and by her enthusiasm for and considerable knowledge of the great Italian poets – something obviously not to be met with among his recent female associates in Venice. And once Byron had followed her to Ravenna, eventually (in 1820) bringing about her separation from her husband, he felt tied to her by duty as well as love. This, predictably, meant that he then began to find the relationship increasingly restrictive; nevertheless, this was much his longest stable, continuous relationship with any woman. He had begun to confine himself, as he put it with a characteristic awareness of the ambiguities of his situation, to 'the strictest adultery'.

Count Guiccioli's attitude to his wife and Byron has puzzled biographers. For some time he either only half-suspected or was willing to tolerate the affair. Possibly his attitude was affected by the fact that Byron was now a wealthy man. Newstead Abbey was at last sold to Thomas Wildman in 1817 for £94,500 and payment received, after further delays, in February 1819. Byron was also now accepting handsome sums for his poems – in 1821, for instance, Murray paid him £1,525 for cantos three to five of *Don Juan*. Between September and November 1819 the count allowed his wife to go off and live with Byron in Venice and at La Mira. During this time Byron worked on the third and fourth cantos of *Don Juan*. These continue – when the narrator is not discussing something else – the story of Juan's shipwreck on a Greek island, one of the Cyclades, after being the only survivor of the long-boat. Here Haidée, daughter of the fierce Lambro, hides Juan in a cave until her 'piratical papa was cruising', and restores him with 'eggs, fruit, coffee, bread,/With Scio [Chios] wine, and all for love, not money'. Juan is soon strong enough to learn a little Greek from his hostess and to become her lover. The relationship is presented as completely natural – Haidée 'was Passion's child', one 'Made but to love, to feel that she was his/Who was her chosen' and even her name (pronounced 'Haydy' in the poem) comes from a Greek word for 'caress'. Surprisingly, the young lovers are almost exempt from the narrator's caustic undermining wit: unmocked, they can wander by the moonlit sea where

> *They heard the wave's splash, and the wind so low,*
> *And saw each other's dark eyes darting light*
> *Into each other – and beholding this,*
> *Their lips drew near, and clung into a kiss.*

Satire is directed, rather, at readers who cannot accept the naturalness of such love: 'Haidée and Juan were not married, but/The fault was theirs not mine' and so instead of blaming the narrator the chaste reader had better shut the book 'Before the consequences grow too awful;/'Tis dangerous to read of loves unlawful'. Marriage, Byron would claim from his recent experience, was in no way superior to this idyllic if 'unlawful' union.

Byron or his narrator may look benignly on young love and refrain on the whole from undercutting it, but the cruelty of circumstance soon destroys it. At the height of the non-stop party which Haidée and Juan are soon presiding over, Lambro quietly returns. The wit begins to flicker dangerously, if again partly at the expense of the reader:

> *Perhaps you think in stumbling on this feast*
> *He flew into a passion, and in fact*
> *There was no mighty reason to be pleased;*
> *Perhaps you prophesy some sudden act,*
> *The whip, the rack, or dungeon at the least,*
> *To teach his people to be more exact,*
> *And that, proceeding at a very high rate,*
> *He show'd the royal penchants of a pirate.*

'You're wrong!' counters the next stanza – Lambro, 'the mildest manner'd man/That ever scuttled ship or cut a throat', proceeds more deliberately, first questioning revellers who have no idea who he is. The action pauses for reflections on the pirate-chief's character, then returns to the party. There are further asides on the nature of glory and much else – the narrator says his fault is digression, 'Leaving my people to proceed alone/While I soliloquize beyond expression'. But then at last, with the satire again mostly held back, Lambro confronts the lovers. Juan is cut down and bundled off to be sold as a slave in Constantinople. Haidée collapses, dying twelve days later. Now, we are told, the isle is 'desolate and bare', with no human traces but the graves of the strong father and the beautiful daughter, while 'no dirge, except the hollow sea's,/Mourns o'er the beauty of the Cyclades'.

An early Victorian version of the dying Haidée. In Don Juan, *canto four: 'Her handmaids tended, but she heeded not;/ Her father watch'd, she turn'd her eyes away; She recognised no being, and no spot,/ However dear or cherish'd in their day.'*

The British Library 789.f.30

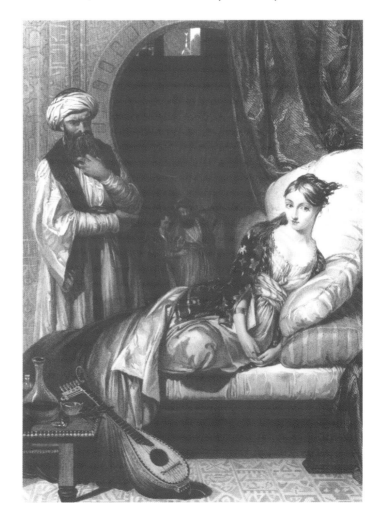

❧ *Ravenna*

Ravenna, the city where Byron spent most of 1820 and 1821, is now well known for its lustrous Byzantine mosaics. These were little to the taste of early nineteenth-century natives or visitors, who tended to prefer their art more approachable, their saints more loving or inspiring than the mosaics' jewelled and confident courtiers and angels. Much more significant as far as Byron was concerned was the tomb of Dante, who had died here in exile in 1321, and the Pineta, the extensive pine-forest (referred to by both Dante and Boccaccio) where he enjoyed almost daily rides.

On the whole Ravenna was a rather sleepy place, 'out of the way of travellers and armies'. For most of his time here Byron lived quietly in an apartment in Palazzo Guiccioli (now Via Cavour 54). When not with the countess he was much alone. He began to eat too much and in early 1821, for the first time since 1816, to keep a journal. In it he writes perhaps with one eye on posterity, but gives at least the impression of remarkable honesty and spontaneity. Topics include politics, indigestion, books, a local woman of ninety-four whom he helped financially, the question of immortality, figures from his English past. Another cure for boredom was the danger of ending 'with a stiletto in my gizzard some fine afternoon'; it was generally suspected that Teresa's husband had arranged more than one convenient death in his time. Work was another distraction – between April 1820 and October 1821 he produced, astonishingly, working mainly at night, a canto of *Don Juan*, five poetic dramas, and *The Vision of Judgement*, a brilliant piece of *ottava rima* satire responding to Southey's poem on the death and apotheosis of George III. (In Byron's version angels and devils flee as the laureate declaims this piece until at line five, unable to endure more, St Peter knocks him down with his keys. In the confusion which follows, the king, in spite of the many wrongs of his long reign, manages to slip into heaven.) And there was also politics, in the shape of Byron's involvement with the local *carbonari* (members of secret societies working for independence from foreign or papal rule), prominent among whom were Teresa's father and brother, the Counts Ruggiero and Pietro Gamba.

Although Count Guiccioli probably knew from near the beginning about the nature of the relationship between Byron and his wife, he did not catch them in a compromising situation until May 1820. He told Byron to leave his house, but took no action when he failed to do so. Peaceful co-existence became easier when the countess left to live with her family. Her father had petitioned the Pope for a separation between the Guicciolis, and this was granted in July. Public opinion was against Count Guiccioli, Byron told Moore, because 'he ought to have cut the matter short *at first*, and not waited twelve months to begin'. Count Giuseppe Alborghetti, who was second only to the Cardinal Legate in the papal government of Ravenna, also looked favourably on Byron, of whose work he was an admirer.

Alborghetti was evidently, as Byron noted in his journal, on 8 January 1821, dealing, 'at present, his cards with both hands'. There was talk of rebellion and he wished to offend neither his papal masters nor the potential – and potentially successful – rebels, who included the Gambas. Byron admired the principles of the carbonari, shared their longing for action, and provided them with what could have been a stronghold or operations centre. In February 1821 when revolution was in the air 'I had furbished up my arms – and got my apparatus ready for taking a turn with the Patriots – having my drawers full of their proclamations – oaths – and resolutions – and my lower rooms of their hidden weapons of most calibres'. Physically courageous as ever, he waited up one night for the call to arms which never came; 'In the mean time, I might as well read as do any thing else, being alone'. But the time was not ripe for insurrection. A rebellion in Naples foundered ignominiously and *carbonari* elsewhere swiftly abandoned their (in any case rather vague) plans. Byron was aware of the vagueness, as of human frailty more generally – now one of the main subjects of his verse. He 'always had an idea that it would be *bungled*'. But even the prospect of 'manly' action had for a time assuaged the frustration of the contemptible 'Cicisbean' (gigolo-like) existence to which, he had told Hobhouse in the summer of 1819, his love for Teresa had consigned him. His loyalty to the Italian cause was unambiguous, as was his preparedness to die for it: 'whatever the sacrifice of individuals, the great cause will gather strength, sweep down what is rugged and fertilize ... what is cultivable' he declared; 'the king-times are finishing' and after bloodshed and tears 'the peoples will conquer in the end'. That he was able thus to

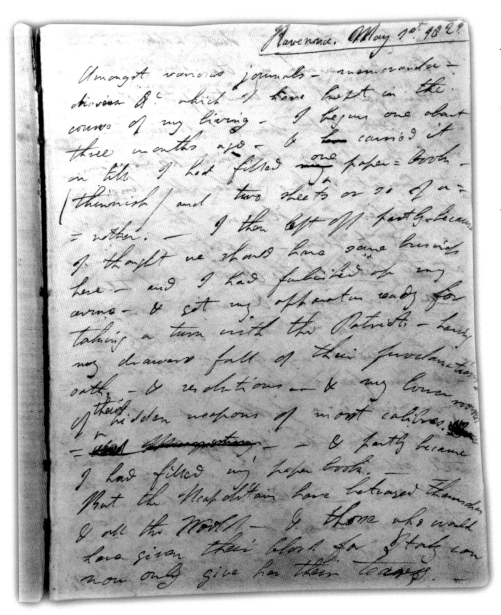

The first page of Byron's 'Ravenna Journal' of 1821. Reflecting at the bottom of the page on the collapse of the projected revolution in Naples, he concludes that 'those who would have given blood for Italy can now only give their tears'.

John Murray

sound more like a French revolutionary than an English aristocrat reflects the degree of political polarisation in a Europe throughout which conservative regimes had tightened their grip on power since the settlement of 1815. It also suggests the differences between Byron's social position in England and in Italy. While in England his rank had been one of the factors which discouraged him from consistent and committed radicalism – his speeches in the House of Lords had been radical but

83

rather isolated performances – here it was possible to be both aristocrat and *carbonaro*, like the Gambas, of whose family he was increasingly becoming a member.

Yet the generalised talk of 'the great cause' and attendant bloodshed is uncharacteristic. On 9 December 1820 the assassination outside Palazzo Guiccioli of Luigi dal Pinto, commandant of the papal troops in Ravenna, affected Byron very differently. He found dal Pinto dying in the street. Since no-one else seemed prepared to help, he had the body carried into the palace. He was much struck by the brute suddenness of the death of this 'brave officer' whom he had often met 'at conversazioni and elsewhere'; it seemed unimportant, by comparison, that one of the 'hidden weapons of most calibres' might soon have been used on such a man. Byron's shock that one so recently 'The foremost in the charge or in the sally,/Should now be butcher'd in a civic alley' at once found a place as a late addition to the fifth canto of *Don Juan*. Reflections already in progress on the puzzling physicality of life, where the functioning of the intellect depends so often on good digestion, are joined by this starker and more immediate illustration of the simple but mystifying facts of life; 'Here we are,/And there we go: – but *where*? five bits of lead,/Or three, or two, or one send very far!' Life breaks in on the poem as death breaks in on life.

Byron sent Canto five to Murray at the end of December 1820. Work on *Don Juan* did not resume until early 1822, mainly, it seems, because of a promise to Teresa to abandon altogether the scandalous poem. (She had read the first two cantos in a French translation.) In the meantime his most notable work was *Cain: a Mystery*, an exploration of the biblical story of Cain's killing of his brother Abel. Cain here is restless, intelligent, and unwilling simply to accept the justice of God's visitation of the sins of the fathers – in this case his parents, Adam and Eve, expelled from Paradise – on the sons and daughters. He is too independent to be won over totally by the persuasive Lucifer (derived partly from Satan in Milton's *Paradise Lost* and Mephostophiles in Goethe's *Faust*). He does, however, begin to question the divine dispensation because of what Lucifer reveals to him: the nature of death and the existence of a pre-Adamite world already destroyed by God. (Here Byron draws on the ideas of Baron Léopold Cuvier, who in 1812 had explained fossils as traces of life before Adam.) Cain kills his unquestioning and submissive brother, Byron told Moore, 'in a fit of dissatisfaction, partly with the politics of Paradise, which had driven them all out of it, and partly because (as it is written in Genesis) Abel's sacrifice was the more acceptable to the Deity'.

Given the subject, the evident scepticism about traditional religious certainties, and Byron's reputation for levity, impiety, and self-projection, it was predictable that some reviewers would be eager to cry blasphemy and to cast the author simply as Cain or Lucifer. Other readers, however, were from the beginning prepared to find something more interesting. *The Monthly Magazine* for February 1822 argued (like the poet himself) that putting into characters' mouths 'the old puzzles of necessity and free will, the origin of evil, and other venerable and inevitable dilemmas' does not make the author irreligious; if he was to be blamed for Lucifer's ideas then Milton – now untouchably respectable – was to be blamed for Satan's. Tom Moore found it 'wonderful – terrible – never to be forgotten'; 'while many may shudder at its blasphemy, all must fall prostrate before its grandeur'. *Cain*, like Byron's other plays or dramatic poems, is avowedly not intended for the stage; the poor reception given to *Marino Faliero* when it was performed in London against his wishes in 1821 confirmed the author in this view. But there have been some successful productions of *Cain*, including one for the Royal Shakespeare Company, adapted and directed by John Barton, in 1995. Audiences, not just readers as Byron expected, have been interested by the difficult questions posed by the honest Cain and eloquent Lucifer.

Pisa, Genoa, the later cantos of Don Juan

In July 1821 the Gambas, father and son, were banished from the Romagna for their dangerous liberalism. (The authorities evidently hoped that the perhaps even more dangerously liberal English lord would soon follow his friends.) They settled in Florence and Teresa Guiccioli was persuaded to join them; the terms of her separation prohibited her from living openly with Byron and if she stayed in Ravenna without her family she ran the risk of being forcibly consigned to a convent. But, happy enough with his way of life in Ravenna and congenitally likely to fall into a routine, her lover lingered on at Palazzo Guiccioli until the end of October. His eventual choice of destination, Pisa, had been strongly influenced by Shelley, who came alone to Ravenna in August. Once more the poets talked through the night. Shelley reported to his wife that Byron 'has ... completely recovered his health, and lives a life totally the reverse of that which he led at Venice. He has a permanent sort of liaison with Contessa Guiccioli. ...'

Shelley, already established in Pisa, arranged for Byron a lease on Palazzo Lanfranchi (now Palazzo Toscanelli), a spacious Renaissance house on the north bank of the Arno. Teresa and her family were accommodated nearby. Pisa would become, Mary Shelley hoped, a 'nest of singing birds'. One of the birds was intended to be the poet and editor Leigh Hunt, whom Byron had visited in 1813 during his spell in prison for libelling the Prince Regent; the plan, nominally Byron's but essentially Shelley's, was that they and Hunt should 'go shares ... in a periodical work, to be conducted here'. (Shelley did not in fact intend to participate, but wanted to bring the others together, not least because the famous poet's share would generate profits which would help Hunt's finances.) But Hunt was long delayed from leaving England by weather, his wife's poor health, and the need for cash. Those who did participate in the Pisan circle, apart from Byron and Shelley, included Edward John Trelawny, a dramatic, black-bearded figure who liked others to believe that he had been a pirate and avowedly modelled himself on Byron's Corsair; John Taaffe, Irish author of a commentary on Dante which Byron recommended to Murray; Thomas

Edward John Trelawny (1792-1881), by Joseph Severn, 1838. Trelawny's entertaining but often unreliable memories of Shelley and Byron were published in Adventures of a Younger Son *(1831) and* Records of Shelley, Byron, and the Author *(1858).*

National Portrait Gallery

Medwin, Shelley's second cousin, who later published *Conversations of Lord Byron*; Edward Williams, once Medwin's fellow army-officer in India, now a friend of Shelley, with whom he and Jane Williams shared accommodation at Tre Palazzi Chiesa, on the south bank of the Arno. All of them were, even if they were Shelley's friends, deeply interested in Byron. Williams, on meeting him, registered surprise that he seemed not haughty or melancholy, as he had expected, but 'all sunshine and good humour'; 'the elegance of his language and the brilliancy of his wit cannot fail to inspire all those who are near him'. Medwin remembered his eyes as greyish brown, peculiarly clear and 'when animated possessed [of] a fire which seemed to look through and penetrate the thoughts of others, while they marked the inspirations of his own'. Meeting the famous or notorious figure they were often anxious to be liked by him and eager to collect information about him (whether for the benefit of posterity or as more immediate gossip) – to discover him for instance, as did Medwin one morning, breakfasting on strong green tea and an egg-yolk and declaring that he lived on claret and soda-water. (Old friends coming to Pisa commented on how fat he had become, while in Genoa a year later he was strikingly thin; he was going through another period of eating disorders. No doubt he also enjoyed watching the reactions of people like Medwin when he told them about his dietary regime.)

The amount of interest in Byron was one factor in the deterioration of his relationship with Shelley during their months together in Pisa. Shelley participated enthusiastically in Byron's favourite pistol shooting, which took place at a farm outside the city. But he was less able or willing to share in the late-night 'man of the world' talk, long games of billiards, and heavy drinking at Palazzo Lanfranchi. As in Switzerland six years earlier, he was convinced of Byron's greatness as a poet, and felt

inhibited in his own writing. And he was angry at Byron's treatment of Claire Clairmont, now living in Florence and kept discreetly away from the noble lord when she visited the Shelleys in Pisa. To her Shelley went so far as to speak of a wish to break off this 'detested intimacy'. But Shelley did not want to break the connection at present; he felt that his involvement was essential if Hunt (when he eventually arrived) and Byron were to be brought together in the planned periodical (*The Liberal*, as it became). He would attempt, therefore, to 'preserve the little influence I may have over this Proteus in whom such strange extremes are reconciled'.

Besides, as the last remark perhaps shows, Shelley remained, at least some of the time, subject to the Byronic charisma; this was one reason for wanting to break free. Meanwhile the women had less chance than usual to experience or resist the attraction. While the men rode, shot, drank and talked, Mary Shelley, Jane Williams and Teresa Guiccioli were left mostly to their own devices. The situation was particularly difficult for the countess who, though she liked Mrs Shelley, found her dauntingly intellectual.

Life for some of the Pisan colonists was, then, less than satisfactory. And in March 1822 an incident took place which suggested that the city could not, besides, long remain their gathering place. One evening as they paused while riding towards one of the gates of the city, Byron, Shelley, Trelawny, Pietro Gamba and others were involved in a scuffle with Stefano Masi, a garrison sergeant-major who was galloping back for roll-call. After an altercation at the gate in which Shelley was unhorsed and Gamba struck at Masi with his riding-crop, the soldier made off only to be stabbed some time later with a pitchfork by Byron's coachman, Vincenzo Papi, as Masi passed Palazzo Lanfranchi. Papi was arrested together with his fellow-servant, the more wild-looking former gondolier Tita Falcieri. For some days it was thought that Masi would die. The foreigners were interviewed by the authorities, and there was much feeling against them in the garrison and in Pisa more generally. Masi recovered and the coachman was soon released, but Tita, his huge black beard having been shaved off, was banished from Tuscany. (He was later able to re-enter his master's service in Genoa.) The whole affair precipitated the break-up of the Pisan circle. The Shelleys left for Lerici, on the Bay of Spezia, soon after the death of Allegra in April. In May

Byron and Teresa Guiccioli went to spend the summer at Villa Dupuy in Montenero, near Livorno. In July Ruggiero and Pietro Gamba were banished from Tuscany and settled temporarily in Lucca (then a small separate state). No longer able to live with her family, on returning from Montenero the countess lived openly at Palazzo Lanfranchi. This broke the conditions of her separation, cutting off her allowance and binding Byron yet more closely to 'strictest adultery'.

The group was shattered more finally on 8 July when Shelley and Williams drowned while attempting to cross the Bay of Spezia in a storm. Their open sailing-boat was the *Don Juan*. (Shelley at one point had wanted, more independently, to call it *Ariel*; in the end they kept the Byronic name, but it was, at the Shelleys' insistence, cut out of the sail.) Although Byron did not approve of Shelley's atheism and could not share his idealism, he was shocked by this sudden loss. For Williams he had good words, and of his fellow poet, condemned or ignored in England at this stage, he told Murray firmly 'You are all brutally mistaken about Shelley who was without exception – the *best* and least selfish man I ever knew'. (He seems to have had little or no notion of the negative feelings Shelley had sometimes entertained towards him.) With the living Mary Shelley, relations were more complicated over the next fifteen months. He commiserated with her, regularly visited her, and employed her as a copyist. (She worked on much of *Don Juan*.) But the practical aid he promised was not, on the whole, forthcoming, although he was now increasingly wealthy. (The death of his mother-in-law in January 1822 brought him, by an earlier settlement, some £6000.) But, like her husband, she retained contradictory impressions. The expectation of hearing Shelley answer, she decided, explained 'what would otherwise be an enigma' – why his 'mere presence and voice ... has the power of exciting such deep and shifting emotions within me. For my feelings have no analogy either with my opinion of him, or the subject of his conversation'. Byron-like characters continued to figure persistently in her novels.

In August the resourceful Trelawny organised the cremation of the bodies of Shelley and Williams on the beaches where, in pitiful condition, they had been washed up. (Trelawny also arranged the burial of Shelley's heart at the Protestant Cemetery in Rome, and was eventually, in 1881, buried in the adjacent grave. His highly unreliable but readable memoirs often seek to promote Shelley at Byron's

Following pages:

Shelley's funeral, as imagined in 1889 by the painter Louis Édouard Fournier.

Louis-Edouard Fournier
1889

expense.) After Shelley's cremation Byron, Trelawny, and Leigh Hunt, who had at last arrived in Italy early in July, drove to Viareggio with the ashes. After the horror and emotions of the day, Hunt recalled, they drank heavily and, as they travelled on towards Pisa, sang, laughed, and shouted. 'I even felt a gayety the more shocking, because it was real and a relief'.

Hunt, his wife and their six children had moved into the ground floor of the Lanfranchi. He took the opportunity to observe Byron at close quarters. Rising late after a night of gin and water and *Don Juan*, the poet 'breakfasted; read; lounged about, singing an air, generally out of Rossini, and in a swaggering style, though in a voice at once small and veiled; then took a bath, and was dressed; and coming downstairs, was heard, still singing' in the courtyard. Inside the palace, less relaxingly for their host, Hunt's children ran riot and left marks on the walls; Byron defended his own quarters by posting his bull-dog on the stairs. There were other tensions: Marianne Hunt fairly openly disapproved of Byron's morals, was infuriated by his complaints about the children, and was determined, to the point of rudeness, not to show any deference to a lord. Leigh Hunt, while generally easier to get on with, exhibited some of the same tendencies, was regarded as one of the 'Cockney' school of writers whose work Byron did not admire – Keats and William Hazlitt were other alleged members – and had a habit of asking, without embarrassment, for money. This lifelong habit made Hunt an evident source, at least in 'the light externals of character' for the genially irresponsible Harold Skimpole in Dickens' novel *Bleak House*, 1852-3. Finally, Hunt's politics might have drawn Byron closer to him had he not been, unglamorously, neither an Italian nor an aristocrat. On moving to Genoa in October 1822 Byron was distinctly pleased no longer to be sharing accommodation, however spacious, with this family.

Nevertheless the lord and the 'cockney' did appear together in *The Liberal*. *The Vision of Judgement* was published in the first number on 15 October. *Heaven and Earth*, a sequel to *Cain*, was in the second number. *The Liberal* was published by Leigh Hunt's brother John, who from 1823 superseded John Murray as publisher of all Byron's new work. The breach with Murray as publisher – Byron continued to correspond with him as a friend – resulted essentially from *Don Juan*. Murray had been reluctant to publish the first five cantos. When he read the next three in

manuscript he wrote that 'they were so outrageously shocking that I would not publish them if you were to give me your Estate – Title and Genius – For Heaven's sake revise them – they are equal in talent to any thing you have written. ... Do let us have your good humour again and put Juan in the tone of Beppo'. Murray's caution was understandable. John Hunt's publication of *The Vision* resulted in his prosecution for libel against the present and previous monarch. (He was eventually fined £100 after Byron's death.) For *Don Juan* itself, however, the change of publisher brought advantages. Murray's two instalments of the poem had been priced at 5s. (small octavo), 9s. 6d. (octavo) and 31s. 6d. (quarto, cantos one and two only) and the

'A Noble Poet Scratching up his Ideas' in a cartoon of 1823. The picture on the wall, showing the death of Abel, is a reminder of Byron's poem Cain. *The books on the floor include his* The Vision of Judgement *and* Heaven and Earth.

British Museum

95

number of copies produced was fairly low – 1500 of the second instalment in octavo as against 12000 of *Childe Harold* canto three. But when John Hunt took over he issued not only octavo editions at 9s. 6d. to be bound, by those who could afford them, with the Murray issues, but cheap editions at one shilling. Seventeen thousand copies of cantos six, seven and eight (1823) were issued at this price. (There were also a number of cheap 'pirate' editions by other publishers.) As a result, the Byron scholar William St Clair concludes from his analysis of the figures, '*Don Juan* was affordable by many groups who had played almost no part in the earlier boom, all the middle classes, but also shopkeepers, tradesmen, artisans and other highly-paid manual workers, many of whom were politically active and much more sympathetic to Byron's ideas than his previous readership'.

Those ideas – chiefly that the ruling establishment is riddled with hypocrisy or 'cant' – were delivered with a new forcefulness and conviction in the later cantos. Early in 1822 Byron had taken up work again on *Don Juan* having, he told Murray on 8 July, 'obtained a permission from my Dictatress to continue it'; it soon became clear that he had no intention of observing Teresa's stipulation that the poem should now become 'more guarded and decorous and sentimental'. He had been angered as well as grieved by the deaths of Allegra and Shelley and he directed some of the anger into satire – and sometimes more direct attack – on the conservative establishment in Britain and Europe. Another stimulus was the arrival of Leigh Hunt who – whatever the personal tensions which arose between him and Byron – came full of radical ideas, fresh from English battles over such issues as freedom of expression and freedom of assembly. Thus ignited, Byron now, in Pisa and then from November at Albaro near Genoa, worked with fire and rapidity on the poem he had once said, half meaning it, was intended only 'to giggle and make giggle'. By March 1823 he was working on the sixteenth canto. John Hunt published cantos six to sixteen in four instalments between July 1823 and March 1824.

Cantos seven and eight deliver an indictment of war (at least as practised by the great powers). Juan, having somehow escaped from Constantinople – Byron fails to specify how – finds himself fighting for the Russian army against the Turks at the siege of Ismail on the Danube, a historical event of 1790. Before Juan even arrives on the scene the notion of military glory has been undercut by the narrator, whose

The opening of Don Juan, *canto seven.*

The British Library Ashley MS 5163.

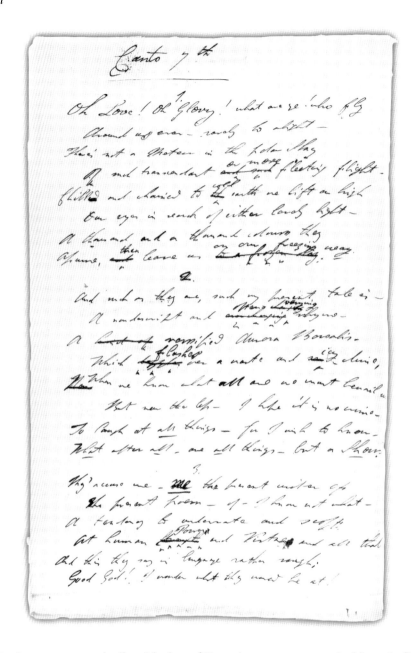

attitude contrasts markedly with that of Byron's pro-war source in Marquis Gabriel de Castelnau's 1820 history of Russia. The Russian general Souvarov, the greatest chief 'That ever peopled hell with heroes slain,/Or plunged a province or a realm in grief', stirs up his men 'Until each high, heroic bosom burned/For cash and conquest'. As often in *Don Juan* serious points emerge from the humour or a moving insight gives way (avoiding 'compassion fatigue') to a different topic: as Ismail falls

The bayonet pierces and the sabre cleaves,
And human lives are lavished every where,
As the year closing whirls the scarlet leaves
When the stript forest bows to the bleak air,
And groans; and thus the peopled City grieves,
Shorn of its best and loveliest, and left bare;
But still it falls with vast and awful splinters,
As Oaks blown down with all their thousand winters.

It is an awful topic – but 'tis not
My cue for any time to be terrific:
For checquered as is seen our human lot
With good, and bad, and worse, alike prolific
Of melancholy merriment, to quote
Too much of one sort would be soporific; –
Without, or with, offence to friends or foes,
I sketch your world exactly as it goes.

King George IV when he was Prince of Wales, as caricatured by James Gillray. 'Though Ireland starve great George weighs twenty stone,' wrote Byron.

Byron addresses his contemporaries – 'your world', the victors of Waterloo in 1815 and the settlement which followed – more than the conquerors of Ismail in 1790. The siege stands for all imperialism. Tsarina Catherine the Great, who thrives on victories and lovers (Juan will for a time join her stable) stands for the rapacious aggression of all monarchs. (Byron is aware, however, that non-monarchic regimes can also be oppressors: 'I wish men to be free/As much from mobs as kings – from you as me'.) There are other outspoken attacks on modern hypocrisy, whether political, sexual, or religious, many of which Murray would have quailed to read, let alone publish. For instance, he writes of the inequities of the Irish famine of 1822, saying 'Though Ireland starve great George [the Fourth] weighs twenty stone' (280 pounds; 'forty stone', says the first draft).

Good, though rare, is not impossible in the world of the Ismail cantos. As the narrator observes, 'The drying up a single tear has more/Of honest fame, than shedding seas of gore'; Juan saves a ten-year-old Turkish girl, Leila, from the

Cossacks (an incident closely based on one in the source) and his deed is allowed to stand, free of cynical asides. She is 'homeless, houseless, helpless' and 'Juan wept/And made a vow to shield her, which he kept'.

In canto ten, after his sojourn with Catherine, Juan arrives in England as her envoy. He remains there for the rest of the poem, giving Byron the opportunity both to expose English high society and somewhat nostalgically to remember his time in its midst. In London and afterwards at Norman Abbey, the idealised version of Newstead lived in by Lord Henry and Lady Adeline Amundeville, description and satire range over balls, dinners, electioneering, fashionable marriages and the administration of local justice. Juan innocently expects England to be governed by noble ideals while the narrator makes clear that it is ruled by the self-interest of 'the twice two thousand for whom earth was made'. They and some of their foreign equivalents need to be locked up; George IV needs to be locked up, or, 'no, not the King, but the Pavilion,/Or else 'twill cost us all another million'. (The exotic palace in Brighton with its oriental domes and furnishings attracted responses as mixed as London's Millennium Dome today.)

These late cantos read, some of the time at least, more like a novel in verse than a mock-epic. Juan's relationships with Lady Adeline, the younger Aurora Raby, and the more straightforwardly sensual Duchess of Fitz-Fulke, are slowly developing as *Don Juan* breaks off after fourteen stanzas of canto seventeen. (Byron told Murray in February 1821 that he intended to make Juan 'a cause for a divorce in England' and 'had not quite fixed whether to have him end in Hell, or in an unhappy marriage, not knowing which would be the severest. The Spanish tradition says Hell: but it is probably only an Allegory of the other state.') Adeline remains the most interesting of the three in the cantos as we have them: she is like a snow-capped volcano or, since that 'tired metaphor' has been used so often by this poet and others,

> *I'll have another figure in a trice:–*
> *What say you to a bottle of champagne?*
> *Frozen into a very vinous ice,*
> *Which leaves few drops of that immortal rain,*
> *Yet in the very centre, past all price,*

About a liquid glassful will remain;

And this is stronger than the strongest grape

Could e'er express in its expanded shape:

'Tis the whole spirit brought to a quintessence;

And thus the chilliest aspects may concentre

A hidden nectar under a cold presence.

356   DON JUAN.

LXXVIII.

To his gay nothings, nothing was replied,
  Or something which was nothing, as urbanity
Required. Aurora scarcely look'd aside,
  Nor even smiled enough for any vanity.

The devil was in the girl! Could it be pride?
  Or modesty, or absence, or inanity?
Heaven knows! But Adeline's malicious eyes
  Sparkled with her successful prophecies,

Aurora Raby, Juan and Adeline, in Don Juan, *from* The Illustrated Byron *(1854).*

The British Library 11611.k.3.

And lest it should be thought that women in *Don Juan* are seen only as bottles of champagne, interestingly frozen or otherwise, he does find room for reflections, serious for a time, on 'the real sufferings of their she condition'.

As the 'tired metaphor' reference suggests, in these late cantos Byron continues to reflect on his own poem, to re-define it. The first twelve cantos, he casually announces at one point, are merely 'preludios' to the work proper; at first it seemed about two dozen cantos would do, but now 'I think to canter gently though a hundred'. He refuses to finish the poem, to limit its length, shape, or direction, just as, so often digressing, he will not limit it to one time-scheme, tone, or range of material. Nothing is excluded; 'He who doubts all things, nothing can deny'. Perhaps the flavour of Don Juan can best be given in this stanza from canto thirteen:

> *I'm 'at my old Lunes' – digression, and forget*   madness
> *The Lady Adeline Amundeville;*
> *The fair most fatal Juan ever met,*
> *Although she was not evil, nor meant ill;*
> *But Destiny and Passion spread the net,*
> *(Fate is a good excuse for our own will)*
> *And caught them; – what do they* not *catch methinks?*
> *But I'm not Oedipus, and life's a Sphinx.*

In Greek myth only Oedipus can answer a riddle propounded by the monstrous sphinx.

While Byron was still working on the last cantos of *Don Juan* he spent much time talking and riding with Marguerite, Countess of Blessington, who later turned her impressions over a ten-week period into a book, *Conversations of Lord Byron* (1832-3). She was 'desirous ... to see "Genoa the Superb"' but attracted still more 'by its being the residence of Lord Byron'. A year younger than he was, she was travelling with her husband and their inseparable companion Count Alfred D'Orsay. D'Orsay made a number of sketches of a Byron now markedly thin as a result of his new starvation diet, and prematurely ageing. The Countess too noticed that his hair was 'getting rapidly grey' and was at first surprised not to find someone 'with a more

dignified and commanding air', the 'hero-looking sort of person' she had always imagined. And Byron himself often spoke now of being tired of passion. In a poem to Lady Blessington of 6 May 1823 he says that once he could have celebrated her beauty in verse as Sir Thomas Lawrence famously had in paint, but 'What I loved I *now* merely admire –/And my heart is as grey as my head'. Yet she found him more lively, puzzling, maddening, and funny than this self-portrait by the ageing thirty-five-year-old suggests. For his part he was delighted to be in the company of a representative of certain aspects of the world he had lost and was remembering, enjoying and attacking in *Don Juan*. ('Ridicule', he told her, is 'the only weapon ... that the English climate cannot rust'.) Blessington herself knew something of the hypocrisy or 'cant' of high society. Although she was at the centre of a respectable male literary circle, it was deemed improper for ladies to mix with her because of her chequered past. At home in Ireland, at the age of fifteen, she had been literally sold to a man by her father; another man had rescued her from that relationship before in turn relinquishing her, for a substantial financial consideration, to the Earl, whose second wife she later became.

Blessington, with her extraordinary range of social experience and convincingly aristocratic ease of manner, felt confident enough to laugh at Byron, and often to make him laugh too, when he hinted at dark secrets in his past, postured in too melancholy a vein, or tried to shock her with his rudeness about absent friends. ('Scandal is so piquant, – it is a sort of cayenne to the mind, – that I confess I like it,' he said to her, 'particularly if the objects are one's particular friends'.) What she found difficult to tolerate, and yet was fascinated by, was his inconsistency, his daily contradictions and mood-shifts and undercutting of his own apparently serious positions with flippancy and self-denigration. He endeavoured to explain himself to her:

> *People take for gospel all I say, and go away continually with false impressions.... I am so changeable, being every thing by turns and nothing long, – I am such a strange* mélange *of good and evil, that it would be difficult to describe me. There are but two sentiments to which I am constant, – a strong love of liberty, and a detestation of cant, and neither is calculated to gain me friends.*

Opposite page:

Marguerite, Countess of Blessington (1789-1849), by Sir Thomas Lawrence. She published several novels and a traval book, The Idler in Italy *(1839), as well as her recollections of Byron's conversation.*

Wallace Collection/ Bridgeman Art Library

While involved with the Blessingtons in the spring of 1823 Byron became deeply interested in the idea of returning to Greece, now in rebellion against its Turkish overlords. Contact with the Blessingtons provided a link with the past and a counterweight to the uncertainty which lay ahead. Lady Blessington could also offer a relaxed non-sexual friendship very different from the emotionally demanding relationship with Teresa Guiccioli. As if to prove the point, Teresa jealously disliked the friendship. Byron was still attached to her but was clearly experiencing some greyness of heart and hair – not a turning against her but a tiredness, an increased awareness of the gap in their ages, and a new liking for solitude. Greece would enable him both to avoid her and to avoid any definite rupture with her. (Helpfully, the Gambas' exile from Ravenna was rescinded. Teresa, after unsuccessfully begging her lover to take her with him to Greece or not to go at all, would accompany her father home; Byron seems genuinely to have felt that it would be better for her in the long run if her husband took her back, although she felt strongly otherwise.) By going to Greece he could also be rid of his irksome commitment to *The Liberal*.

For personal reasons, therefore, he listened very willingly when Edward Blaquière of the London Greek Committee flatteringly encouraged him to lend his aid in 'resuscitating the land already so well illustrated by your sublime and energetic muse'. There were also, of course, more noble reasons for going to the aid of the Greeks. Prominent among these were the 'love of liberty' – for the oppressed as well as for himself – which he had proclaimed to Lady Blessington and the love of Greece in particular which he had imbibed in 1809-11. The rebellion had begun in 1821 and attracted the interest of both Byron and Shelley, in whose *Hellas* 'Greece and her foundations are/Built beneath the tide of war,/Based on the crystalline sea/Of thought and its eternity'. Byron, with his practical experience of the country and cynicism about human nature, was better equipped actually to participate in the conflict. (Philhellenic volunteers who lacked this necessary hard-headedness and expected to find every Greek an ancient hero were already returning in droves to western and northern Europe.) Yet he was not lacking, as he had shown in his thoughts on the possibility of insurrection in Ravenna, in idealism. Already in the third canto of *Don Juan* he had included the song 'The isles of Greece ...'. This fast became almost an anthem for lovers of Greece, especially the lines referring to the ancient victory of the Greeks at Marathon:

The mountains look on Marathon –
And the mountains look on the sea;
And musing there an hour alone,
I dream'd that Greece might still be free;
For standing on the Persians' grave,
I could not deem myself a slave.

Once Byron had been elected to the London Greek Committee in May there was no easy going back. To friends in Genoa he seemed by turns enthusiastic about and contemptuous of the whole Greek project. Just before his final departure he told his Genoa banker Charles Barry that he would turn back even then but that 'Hobhouse and the others would laugh at him'. (Hobhouse, now a liberal member of parliament, was also on the Committee.) But the Committee, smaller and less influential at this stage than Byron realised, needed him badly. His very famous name (and his money) would count for much. And he also felt that Greece, and quite possibly death there, was his destiny. It might end his sufferings, perhaps redeem his reputation in England, and enable him at last to shine not in ink but in deeds.

Byron's cavalry helmet and other artefacts belonging to him and his associates, made in Genoa by Giacomo Aspe for the expedition to Greece, 1823.

Newstead Abbey

〰 *Greece*

In mid-July the rolling, slow moving brig *Hercules* eventually left Genoa. On board were Byron, Trelawny, Pietro Gamba, other companions, crew-members, horses, the poet's bulldog Moretto and his newfoundland Lyon, stores, arms and money. As usual Byron talked freely about his friends, lovers and wife, yet impressed people as sociable and, for all his denigration of others, fundamentally benign. As they passed Stromboli, off Sicily, the poet spent some of the night contemplating the volcano and even told Trelawny 'If I live another year, you will see this scene in a fifth canto of *Childe Harold*'. In a different if no less characteristic mood he indulged in such pranks as taking the portly captain's best scarlet waistcoat for a sea-outing: Byron and Trelawny swam each with one arm in the capacious garment.

On 3 August the *Hercules* put in at Argostoli on Cephalonia, one of the seven islands which formed the British Protectorate of the Ionian Isles. The High Commissioner of the protectorate, Sir Thomas Maitland, was careful to observe official British neutrality in the conflict just across the water between the Greeks and Turks. On Cephalonia, however, Byron could usefully consult the Resident, Colonel Charles James Napier, a level-headed military man who was also, to Maitland's disgust, an evident philhellene. Napier confirmed what Byron feared, that the Greek leaders were at daggers drawn with each other as much as the Turks. There were rival local power bases on the island of Hydra, in the Peloponnese and elsewhere. The two principal factions were at this point those led by Prince Alexandros Mavrokordatos, a returned exile, and the southern warlord Theodoros Kolokotronis. In November the London Greek Committee sent out Colonel Leicester Stanhope, a disciple of Jeremy Bentham the Utilitarian (proponent of 'the greatest happiness of the greatest number'). Byron and Napier worked patiently to try to persuade him that Greek problems would not easily be solved by correct thinking, the establishment of printing presses, and institutional reform. Unsuitable equipment as well as unsuitable people arrived; from Cephalonia in December Byron wrote to John Bowring of the Committee to explain politely that the supplies were 'occasionally hardly *practical* enough – in the present state of

Greece – for instance the Mathematical instruments are thrown away – none of the Greeks know a problem from a poker – we must conquer first – and plan afterwards. – The use of the trumpets, too, may be doubted ...'. It was necessary to understand the real situation on the mainland before the Committee's or Byron's money was dispensed to the groups and individuals who were already busy asking for it: to understand that 'whoever goes into Greece at present should do it as Mrs Fry [the prison reformer] went into Newgate – not in the expectation of meeting with any especial indication of existing probity – but in the hope that time and better treatment will reclaim the present burglarious and larcenous tendencies which have followed this general gaol delivery'. Nevertheless he agreed to lend the provisional government in western Greece £4000. But, still avoiding too clear commitment to one faction, he continued to bide his time on the island. Trelawny saw this simply as vacillation and left to seek active service in the Peloponnese.

While Trelawny was still with Byron they occupied themselves by visiting Ithaca, where, as Trelawny remembered, verdant valleys and sparkling streams contrasted with 'the arid wastes and barren red hills of Cephalonia'. They saw some of the sites traditionally associated with Homer's Odysseus, although, probably exaggerating, Trelawny says that Byron wanted to go for a swim instead since, as Byron claimed, 'I detest antiquarian twaddle. Do people think I have no lucid intervals, that I came to Greece to scribble more nonsense?' But back at the small villa at Metaxata, on Cephalonia, which Byron shared with Trelawny and Gamba, there were moments of peace such as he had rarely experienced. On 17 October 1823 he temporarily resumed his journal because

> *standing at the window of my apartment in this beautiful village – the calm though cool serenity of a beautiful and transparent Moonlight – showing the Islands – the Mountains – the Sea – with a distant outline of the Morea [Peloponnese] traced between the double Azure of the waves and skies – have quieted me enough to be able to write – which (however difficult it may seem for one who has written so much publicly – to refrain) is and always has been to me – a task and a painful one.*

Such feelings did not, however, find expression in verse, and most of Byron's letters from Greece, while often lively, are concerned above all with practical matters. He writes to Hobhouse not only as an old friend but as a member who must report his findings to the Committee. Writing to Teresa Guiccioli he is often rather perfunctory, his expressions of love perhaps rather forced; sometimes he simply adds a postscript to Gamba's letters to her.

Italy and Teresa seemed remote. Much of Byron's time was now spent in male company. His final love was for Loukas Khalandritsanos, a youth of fifteen whose family, refugees on Ithaca, he had helped and settled in Argostoli. Loukas became his page and accompanied him when, at the end of 1823, he set out to join Mavrokordatos – while still hoping not to be associated too closely with him – in the strategically important mainland town of Missolonghi. He would, Mavrokordatos assured him, be 'received as a saviour'. During the crossing Byron's party was nearly captured by a Turkish ship. Byron had feared the worst for Loukas. He told Stanhope: 'I would sooner cut him in pieces and myself too than have him taken out by those barbarians'.

In Missolonghi on 3 January 1824 Byron was given a hero's welcome. But from the first there were frustrations. The setting was unhealthy – the town was almost surrounded by stagnant lagoons and there was much heavy rain; Byron called the place a 'mud-basket'. The Turkish blockade, broken for a time, was soon re-imposed and opportunities for engaging the enemy were continually thwarted. He was bombarded with demands for money and mediation from Greeks and volunteers of every faction. He had employed as soldiers several hundred Suliotes – Albanian warriors of the sort he had met in 1809 and celebrated in *Childe Harold* canto two – but found them quarrelsome, money-grabbing and dishonest. On more than one occasion only his coolness in crisis seems to have stopped them from pillaging the town. Loukas made him, no doubt, think longingly of his relationship with John Edleston the choirboy, but this time the love was unrequited. Byron's powerful physical attractiveness was, he felt, at last beginning to fade. But out of this situation came his last few poems. In one, not published until 1887 and now known as 'Love and Death', he traces his unwavering devotion to Loukas 'when the foe was at our side' and

on other occasions; when Byron had a near fatal convulsive seizure on 15 February his spirit turned to Loukas 'even in the grasp of death';

> *Thus much and more – and yet thou lov'st me not,*
> *And never wilt – Love dwells not in our will –*
> *Nor can I blame thee – though it be my lot*
> *To strongly – wrongly – vainly – love thee still.*

The better-known poem headed 'January 22nd 1824. Messalonghi. On this day I complete my thirty sixth year' (published later in 1824) begins from a desire to go on loving although ''Tis time the heart should be unmoved/Since others it hath ceased to move'. But, shown to the upright Stanhope, the idealistic Gamba and others as soon as it was written, this poem was meant more for public consumption than 'Love and Death'. Here and now in Greece, 'Where glory decks the hero's

Byron's house in Missolonghi. Edward John Trelawny, who arrived in Missolonghi a few days after Byron's death, described the town as 'situated ... on the verge of the most dismal swamp I have ever seen. The marvel was that Byron, prone to fevers, should have been induced to land on this mudbank, and stick there for three months shut in by a circle of stagnant pools which might be called the belt of death.'

The British Library 841.m.20

George Gordon, Lord Byron

*The first page of
Byron's 'On this day
I complete my thirty-
sixth year'.*

*The British Library
Add MS 31038*

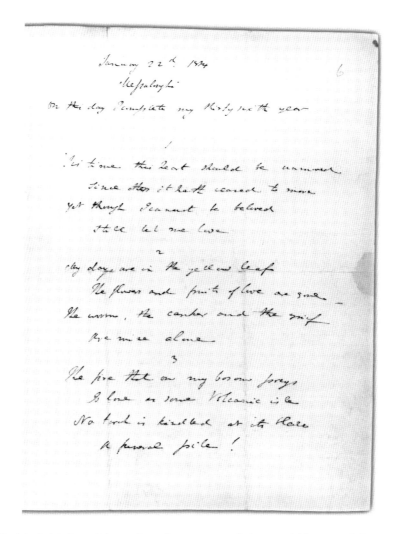

bier/Or binds his brow', love-thoughts are out of place and 'those reviving passions'
unworthy of manhood must be trodden down;

Awake! (not Greece – She is awake!)
Awake my spirit ...

Seek out – less often sought than found,
A Soldier's Grave – for thee the best,
Then look around and choose thy ground
And take thy Rest.

Byron playing with his
newfoundland, Lyon,
an illustration to
William Parry's The
Last Days of Lord
Byron, *1825.*
The figures in the
background are
members of Byron's
Suliote regiment.

The British Library
1164.g.25

In Missolonghi Byron rode, shot, wrote letters, waited on the loan from the Committee that he was intended to administer (it was finalised just before his death), and adjudicated in disputes over rank and precedence among the volunteers. He talked and drank with the 'fine rough subject' the 'fire-master' or artillery expert

William Parry, who shared his practical grasp of the Greeks' problems and the problematic Greeks. During these months Byron also arranged the release of a number of captive Turkish women and, like Juan rescuing Leila at Ismail, took care of a nine-year-old Turkish girl, Hatadje, and her mother: rare good deeds amid the savagery of the Greek War of Independence.

The convulsions he had experienced in February were the prelude to his final collapse. On 9 April, having ridden in heavy rain, he developed a fever. The following morning he rode again. Over the next few days the fever worsened, no doubt exacerbated by recent stresses and by a lifetime of hard drinking and erratic dieting. His doctors, Francesco Bruno and Julius Millingen, both inexperienced, were near to panic. Bleeding was the only remedy they had much faith in; their patient, aware that 'the lancet had killed more people than the lance', resisted for days before eventually giving in. It seems likely that loss of blood at least hastened his decline. In a house of confused, shocked, weeping people – the calmer Parry said that Gamba, Fletcher and Dr Bruno 'required almost as much attention and assistance as Lord Byron himself' – the patient drifted in and out of consciousness. He expressed readiness to die, 'for to terminate my wearisome existence I came to Greece', but was frustrated not to have made a final visit to England first. He spoke of his daughter Ada, his wife and sister, sent Loukas money, mentioned Clare (the Earl of Clare, no doubt, rather than Claire Clairmont). In delirium he thought that at last he was leading his men into action. More characteristically in one lucid moment, holding the hand of the weeping Tita Falcieri, he said, half smiling, 'Oh questa è una bella scena' ('Oh this is a fine scene'). At another point, according to Dr Millingen, the Byron of religious scepticism mixed with strong residual faith – the author of *Cain* – made a last appearance in words which might have been spoken by Mozart's Don Giovanni: '"Shall I sue for mercy?" Then, after a pause, he answered himself: "Come, come, no weakness! Let's be a man to the last".'

On the evening of 18 April Byron said 'I want to sleep now'. He did not wake again, dying at 6 p.m. on 19 April. 'A Soldier's Grave' was not to be had, but his death drew attention to the Greek cause, inspiring an important new wave of foreign support. He passed into Greek legend as a hero, publicly mourned, commemorated in statues, paintings, road-names, personal names.

🖋 *Epilogue*

Against Byron's own wishes his body was dissected by the doctors, who were eager to inspect the anatomy of genius and to investigate the deformed foot. He had wanted to be buried without fuss where he died, but his body was sent back to England and eventually, in July, placed in the family vault in the church at Hucknall Torkard, near Newstead.

Many people were affected by his death. His wife, her bitterness briefly qualified by sorrow, insisted on a detailed account of the last days from William Fletcher. Teresa Guiccioli recovered to promote and enjoy her reputation as Byron's lover (even after marrying a French marquis in 1840) for her remaining fifty-five years. Mary Shelley told Trelawny that 'He could be hardly called a friend – but connected with him in a thousand ways, admiring his talents and with all his faults feeling affection for him, it went to my heart when the other day the hearse that

The meeting of Byron and Walter Scott (on the right) at Albemarle Street in 1815. The fireplace is the one in which Byron's memoirs were burnt.
Painting by L. Werner, c.1850.

John Murray

contained his lifeless form, a form of beauty which in life I often delighted to behold, passed my window going up Highgate Hill on his last journey'. Hobhouse was among the most deeply grieved, and remained his friend's loyal defender until his own death in 1869. Unfortunately he saw it as his duty to his friend's reputation to ensure the destruction of his memoirs; Byron had given the manuscript to Moore in two parts in 1819-20, but Hobhouse and Murray persuaded him, in spite of his better judgement, to allow it to be burnt in Murray's fireplace at 50 Albemarle Street. (The memoirs, Byron had told Murray, omitted 'all my *loves*' but included 'many opinions, and some fun, with a detailed account of my marriage and its consequences, as true as a party concerned can make such accounts, for I suppose we are all prejudiced'.) But much else of Byron's personal and poetic legacy survived to challenge, outrage and delight posterity.

The Danish sculptor Bertel Thorvaldsen 'has done a bust of me at Rome for Mr Hobhouse – which is reckoned very good', Byron wrote to his publisher, John Murray, in June 1817. Hobhouse had wanted his friend's head to be crowned with the traditional poet's laurel wreath but the sitter vetoed this idea; it would be presumptuous and besides 'I won't have my head garnished like a Christmas pie with holly - or a cod's head and fennel'.

John Murray

George Gordon, Lord Byron 1788-1824

⨯ *Chronology*

1788	22 January	Birth of George Gordon Byron, son of John Byron (1756-91) and Catherine Gordon Byron (1765-1811), in Holles Street, London.
1789		Byron and his mother move to Aberdeen. French Revolution begins.
1791	August	Death of John Byron.
1793	January	Louis XVI of France guillotined.
1794-8		Byron is a pupil at Aberdeen Grammar School.
1798	May	On the death of his great-uncle, succeeds as 6th Lord Byron.
	August	Leaves Scotland and begins first period at Newstead Abbey, Nottinghamshire.
1799-1801		Pupil at Dr Glennie's school, Dulwich.
1801-5		Pupil at Harrow.
1803	Summer	Falls in love with Mary Chaworth.
1805	October	Begins residence at Trinity College, Cambridge. At Cambridge he meets friends including John Cam Hobhouse and forms a relationship with the chorister John Edleston.
1806	November	*Fugitive Pieces* printed privately.
1807	January	*Poems on Various Occasions* printed privately.
	June	*Hours of Idleness* published.
	October	'British Bards' (early sketch for *English Bards and Scotch Reviewers*) begun.
	December	Leaves Cambridge. (He is awarded the degree of MA in 1808).
1808		Much involved in dissipation, mostly in London, in Brighton, and at Newstead.
	March	William Fletcher enters Byron's service.
1809	March	Byron takes his seat in the House of Lords. First edition of *English Bards and Scotch Reviewers* published.
1809-11		Byron's Grand Tour. With Hobhouse he visits Portugal, Spain, Gibraltar, Malta (where he has a brief but intense affair with Constance Spencer Smith), Greece, Albania, and Turkey. Hobhouse returns to England in July 1810. Byron spends a second period in Greece until April 1811.
1811	July	Arrives back in England
	August	Death of Catherine Gordon Byron.
	November	Byron introduced to Thomas Moore by Samuel Rogers.
1812	February	Byron speaks in the House of Lords for the first time, on the 'Frame-Breaking' bill.
	March	Publication of cantos I and II of *Childe Harold's Pilgrimage*.

	April	Speaks in the House of Lords on the Catholic Claims bill. Begins affair with Lady Caroline Lamb (until late summer).
	September	Begins work on *The Giaour*.
	October	First marriage proposal to Annabella Milbanke (through Lady Melbourne) rejected.
	December	Begins affair with Lady Oxford (until June 1813)
1813	June	Third and final speech in the House of Lords.
		The Giaour (first edition) published; revised and extended in four further editions between now and September.
	Summer	By now sexual involvement with half-sister Augusta Leigh has begun.
	November	Writes *The Bride of Abydos*.
	December	*The Bride of Abydos* published.
		Writes *The Corsair*.
1814	February	*The Corsair* published; sells 10,000 copies on the first day.
	April	Byron writes 'Ode to Napoleon Buonaparte' following the Emperor's abdication.
		Birth of Elizabeth Medora Leigh, possibly Byron's daughter.
	August	*Lara* published.
	September	Proposes again to Annabella Milbanke and is accepted.
1815	January	Marriage of Byron and Milbanke.
	March	Napoleon returns to France.
	April	*Hebrew Melodies* published.
	May	Byron becomes a member of the Management Sub-Committee of Drury Lane Theatre.
	June	Battle of Waterloo.
	October	Writes *The Siege of Corinth*.
	December	Birth of the Byrons' daughter Augusta Ada.
1816	January	Byron's wife and daughter leave London. He never sees them again. A formal separation is agreed in April.
	February	*The Siege of Corinth* published.
	March	Writes 'Fare Thee Well!'
	April	Leaves England.
	May	Visits Waterloo and begins *Childe Harold* canto III (finished in late June).
		Travels through Germany to Switzerland.
	June	Settles at Villa Diodati on Lake Geneva. Percy Bysshe Shelley, Mary Godwin and Claire Clairmont are established nearby.
		Writes 'The Prisoner of Chillon' (published December).
	September	While touring the Bernese Oberland with Hobhouse, Byron writes his 'Alpine Journal'.
		Begins *Manfred*.
	October-November	Travels through northern Italy to Venice.
	November	*Childe Harold* canto III published.
		Affair with Marianna Segati (until March 1818).

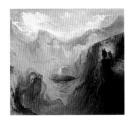

1817	January	Birth of Allegra, Byron's daughter by Claire Clairmont.
	February	Finishes *Manfred*; re-writes Act Three in April, however.
	April-May	Visits Rome.
	June	*Manfred* published.
		Begins *Childe Harold* canto IV (first draft finished by late July).
	August	Meets Margarita Cogni; affair with her lasts probably until the end of 1818.
	October	Completes *Beppo*.
1818	January	Meets Countess Teresa Guiccioli.
	February	*Beppo* published.
	April	*Childe Harold* canto IV published.
	July	Begins *Don Juan* canto I (finished September).
	August	Shelley visits Byron in Venice and rides with him on the Lido.
	December	Byron works on *Don Juan* canto II.
1819	February	Receives money from the sale of Newstead Abbey.
	April	Falls in love with Teresa Guiccioli.
	June-September	In Ravenna and Bologna with Teresa Guccioli and her husband.
	June	*Mazeppa* published.
	July	Publication of *Don Juan* cantos I-II.
	October-November	Works on *Don Juan* canto III (divided into two cantos early in 1820).
	December	Byron settles in Ravenna.
1820	February	Rents upper floor of Palazzo Guiccioli in Ravenna.
	April	Begins work on *Marino Faliero* (finished July).
	July	Teresa Guiccioli and her husband separate.
	August	Byron initiated into the Carbonari (secret revolutionary society).
	October-November	Works on *Don Juan* canto V.
	December	Assassination of Luigi dal Pinto, commandant of papal troops in Ravenna.
1821	January-February	Byron keeps a 'Ravenna Journal'.
		Begins tragedy *Sardanapalus* (finished May).
	April	*Marino Faliero* published and, against the author's will, staged at Drury Lane.
	May	Begins work on *The Vision of Judgement* (completed in October).
	July	Begins *Cain*.
	August	Shelley visits Byron in Ravenna.
		Don Juan cantos III-V published.
	October	Begins the journal 'Detached Thoughts' (until May 1822).
		Begins *Heaven and Earth*.
	November	Settles at Casa Lanfranchi, Pisa.
	December	Publication of *Cain* and *Sardanapalus*.

1822	March	Byron, Shelley, Trelawny and others involved in altercation with sergeant-major Masi. Afterwards Masi is wounded and Byron's servant Tita Falcieri arrested and banished.
	April	Death of Allegra.
	May-July	Byron and Teresa Guiccioli at Villa Dupuy, Montenero, near Livorno.
	July	Leigh Hunt arrives in Pisa.
		Shelley and Edward Williams drowned.
		Byron resumes work on *Don Juan*. Between now and May
1823		he completes cantos VI-XVI.
	October	Settles at Albaro, Genoa.
		The Vision of Judgement published in *The Liberal*.

1823	January	*Heaven and Earth* published in *The Liberal*.
	April	Meets Lady Blessington, seeing her often until she leaves Genoa in June.
		Agrees to become a member of the London Greek Committee.
	May	Begins the unfinished *Don Juan* canto XVII.
		Begins preparations to go to Greece.

	July	Cantos VI-VIII of *Don Juan* published by John Hunt following Byron's breach with his regular publisher John Murray. Hunt will publish the remaining instalments of the poem.
		Byron sails for Greece.

	August	Reaches Cephalonia, where he remains, apart from a brief visit to Ithaca, until near the end of December.
		Don Juan cantos IX-XI published.
	November	Agrees loan of £4000 to the Greek Provisional Government.
	December	*Don Juan* cantos XII-XIV published.
		By the end of the year Loukas Khalandritsanos has become Byron's page - and the subject of his unrequited love.

1824	January	Joins Prince Alexandros Mavrokordatos at Missolonghi on the Greek mainland.
		Writes 'January 22nd 1824. Messalonghi. On this day I complete my thirty sixth year'.
	February	Convulsive fit. Appears gradually to recover.
		Arranges the release of a number of Turkish prisoners.
	March	Cantos XV-XVI of *Don Juan* published.
	April	Byron develops the fever from which, together with the effects of medical bleeding, he dies on 19.
	July	Buried at Hucknall Torkard.

~ *Further Reading*

George Gordon, Lord Byron, *Letters and Journals*, ed. Leslie A. Marchand, 12 vols

(London: John Murray, 1973-82)

Lord Byron: the Complete Poetical Works, ed. Jerome J. McGann and Barry Weller, 7 vols

(Oxford: Oxford University Press, 1980-91)

BIOGRAPHY

Leslie A. Marchand, *Byron: a Biography*, 3 vols

(London: John Murray, 1957; revised and abridged as *Byron: a Portrait*, 1970)

Phyllis Grosskurth, *Byron: the Flawed Angel*

(London: Houghton Mifflin, 1997)

Benita Eisler, *Byron: Child of Passion, Fool of Fame*

(London: Hamish Hamilton, 1999)

Byron: Interviews and Recollections, ed. Norman Page

(Basingstoke: Macmillan, 1985)

Norman Page, *A Byron Chronology*

(Basingstoke: Macmillan, 1988; Boston: G.K. Hall, 1988)

OTHER IMPORTANT STUDIES

Anne Barton, 'Byron and the Mythology of Fact', Nottingham Byron Lecture

(Nottingham, 1968)

Anne Barton, *Don Juan*

(Cambridge: Cambridge University Press, 1992)

Caroline Franklin, *Byron's Heroines*

(Oxford: Clarendon Press, 1992)

Louis Crompton, *Byron and Greek Love: Homophobia in 19th-Century England*

(London: Faber, 1985)

William St Clair, 'The Impact of Byron's Writings: an Evaluative Approach',

in *Byron: Augustan and Romantic*, ed. Andrew Rutherford

(London: Macmillan, 1990), pp. 1-26

Frances Wilson, ed., *Byromania: Portraits of the Artist in Nineteenth- and Twentieth-Century Culture*

(London and Basingstoke: Macmillan, 1999)

Index

Front cover illustrations:	*Lord Byron*, Newstead Abbey; *Don Juan, canto seven,* Ashley MS 5163, The British Library; *Argostoli on the Greek island of Cephalonia*, engraved by Edward Lear, 1782.d.16, The British Library
Back cover illustrations:	*West view of Newstead Abbey*, Newstead Abbey Lord Byron, 7868.d.15, The British Library
Half title page:	Lord Byron, 7868.d.15, The British Library
Frontispiece:	*Love and Gold*, Ashley MS 4727 f.1, The British Library
Contents page:	*The Greek Island of Cephalonia*, photograph by David Sutherland

Text © 2000 Martin Garrett
Illustrations © 2000 The British Library Board and other named copyright holders

Published in the United States of America by
Oxford University Press, Inc.
198 Madison Avenue
New York, NY 10016
www.oup.com

Oxford is a registered trademark of Oxford University Press, Inc.

ISBN 0-19-521677-6

First published 2000 by The British Library, 96 Euston Road, London NW1 2DB

Designed and typeset by Crayon Design, Stoke Row, Henley-on-Thames
Map by John Mitchell
Colour and black and white origination by Crayon Design and South Sea International Press
Printed in Hong Kong by South Sea International Press